I0109687

# DESIGN
# LOVE
# IN

# DESIGN LOVE IN

## How to Unleash the Most Powerful Force in Business

MARCUS BUCKINGHAM

Harvard Business Review Press • Boston, Massachusetts

Printed in the United States of America

10 9 8 7 6 5 4 3 2 1



Library of Congress Cataloging-in-Publication data is forthcoming.

ISBN: 978-1-64782-991-9
eISBN: 978-1-64782-992-6

The paper used in this publication meets the requirements of the American National Standard for Permanence of Paper for Publications and Documents in Libraries and Archives Z39.48-1992.

*For Myshel, whose love is light, and fire.*

To love a thing means wanting it to live.

**The Analects of Confucius**

Love is the bridge between you and everything.

**Rumi**

Let all that you do be done in love.

**1 Corinthians 16:14**

# Contents

# Prologue: Up Close

This book begins in tears. Yes, this is a leadership book. It is absolutely, I promise, without question, a leadership book. But it may be the first leadership book that begins in tears.

My tears, as it happens. It's 3 a.m. and I am, for the umpteenth time, replaying an experience in my mind. Once again, it is the day I sold my company. I am looking out at the faces of my people. Always the same people. Always the same image. Their faces, me mouthing words. I can't hear what I'm saying—I see only their reactions. All around me the air is heavy with confusion and sadness.

You see, back in 2017, I broke something beautiful.

Not my fault, I keep telling myself. In truth, it was.

Between 2007 and 2017 I built a special sort of company. I took all the research I'd ever been a part of and decided to bet it all on my ability to create a suite of products, and a company to grow them. The company's mission was to help each person find and express their unique strengths using a technology called StandOut. As every entrepreneur knows, the building of a company is an exercise in positive self-talk bordering on delusion. You wake up every day passionately committed to your mission, while at the same time questioning whether you might be the only person in the world who cares about it. Or even understands it.

But then you meet others who seem to move to the beat of the same drum as you. Kevin, and Jaqai, and David, and Tiffany, and Darren, and soon scores of others, all of whom you summon up the courage to ask to join your mission, and all of whom sign on. The momentum builds as we win contracts we have no right to win, and deliver tech that a few months prior we couldn't even envision.

You're still worried, of course—scanning the balance sheet, wondering how you'll make payroll this month, and whether hiring those ten new engineers will be one bridge too far for your cash flow—but you look around and you see how committed the entire team is. They have each other's back. They bring their friends, and even family, into the company ranks. They're wearing company swag on the weekends. We are them and they, in all their beautiful diversity, are us.

It was a truly lovely thing we all made.

And I'm the fool who blew it up.

In 2017 I sold the company to a *Fortune* 100 firm. The sale price was good. My rational calculations were sensible. I wanted the mission to be spread more broadly, more quickly, and what better way to do this than through the acquiring firm's three-thousand-plus salespeople? "We have such a grand mission," I told the company on the day of the sale. "But to make the mission real we need an equally grand number of people committed to it!" I liked the sound of my own words, and on that day, I believed them.

But that day I broke a great many hearts.

The looks of hurt and disappointment—looks that at the time I chalked up to people's natural fear of change—replay nightly in my dreams. Because these looks were prescient. The company of passionate people would soon be split up into different silos within the larger organization. Passion would be pushed down by the banal rituals of corporate life: the performance reviews, the calibration sessions, the cascaded goals, the need to "run this by legal." Little by little the language of love and heart and crazy-level commitment to the customers' experience was lost.

The larger firm wasn't deliberately destructive. It was just relentless in its mild but unremitting focus on the needs of the corporation, and its reduction of each person's humanity to a countable resource—where a person's uniqueness became, in ways large and small, merely an obstacle to compliance.

*What is happening?* I asked myself. *Where did the love go?*

The answer, of course, wasn't that anyone had set out to kill the love, or break the hearts. It was that the larger firm simply had different priorities. Its growth. Its earnings. Its investors. Its risk prevention. These were what it cared about most, and so these were what it talked about most. And enforced. And rewarded.

Love dies, the poet Pablo Neruda reminds us, not from being killed. It dies from forgetting. From neglect.

In most organizations today, hearts break and love dwindles because no one talks about them anymore. They have lost their real-world meaning. They are without use. And so they vanish. What I was witnessing up close and personal was what happens in so many large organizations. The fundamental moral worth of each human was everywhere being replaced with the functional needs of the organization. Every interaction became a transaction. Every human merely a resource. The heart slowly bled out, until one day no one could remember what it felt like anymore. What makes us human, what makes work worth doing, what makes life worth living, was gone. Right in front of me. This beautiful thing we'd made died.

Looking at the broken-down people and the disintegrated parts of my company, I realized how much I'd lost. How cavalier I'd been. How all it takes for the light of a company to go out is for its leaders to look away. To ignore its source. To value investor outcomes and devalue the rest.

And it woke me up.

Well, first it destroyed me. Nights of self-recrimination. *How could I have been so stupid?!*

And then it woke me up.

God knows I love data, but sometimes the heart can break open the data—examining data through the lens of the heart can reveal hidden patterns and glossed-over truths. So, broken-hearted, I went back to all my research files and reevaluated the data. What was it precisely that I had seen disappearing? How had we nourished it as we were building my company, and how did it dry out when I sold it? What had come to be "acceptable" that the very best leaders would never accept? What disciplines would these leaders commit to and stick to no matter what?

I've been heads down into this research since 2020, this deep-dive review of all the data I've collected over the last quarter century. This book, and the discovery of the foundational leadership skill at its core—Design Love In—is the result.

I don't know what you think of the word *destiny*. I'm coming around to the idea of it. You see, I think I was meant to lose what I lost. Because what happened to my company is happening to all of us. Slowly. Quietly. Systemically. What I lost we are all on the verge of losing. We are letting something beautiful die—not with intent, but with inattention. We are leaders who've forgotten what we're meant to protect. We've stopped talking about love. We've stopped designing for it, measuring for it, standing for it.

We've unchained ourselves from the most powerful force in the world. We've done it in the name of margin, of efficiency, of scale, of safety, of "minimum viable." And it's costing us something we may never be able to get back. I think I was meant to go through that loss so I could see it clearly—and say it plainly—before it disappears from our work, and from our lives, completely.

This book is my attempt to remember. To make the case for us all that love at work isn't sentimental. It is structural, and strategic, and powerful. It's the only way up.

So, this is not just a leadership book. It is, in its way, a stand for what must never be forgotten.

I was meant to write this book now.

You were meant to read it now.

Before we forget.

## Introduction

# What Now Must Leaders Do?

Twenty-five years ago I wrote a book summarizing Gallup's study of eighty thousand great managers. We called it *First, Break All the Rules* because so many of the world's best managers broke so many of the rules of conventional management wisdom. They didn't treat every employee the same. They didn't identify and then correct people's weaknesses. They played favorites. And no, they didn't think you could ever get too close to your people.

I wrote it not just because I loved rigorous research into human behavior and was frustrated that so much management advice was devoid of it. The research had also revealed something deeply human and, to me, inspiring: the best managers in the world saw each person as unique, and all their strategies were, fundamentally, an effort to capitalize on this uniqueness. While so many corporate systems, when laid bare, were designed to grind uniqueness down and make each person conform, the best managers in the world rejected this notion. They saw each human's unique talents as a feature, not a bug. As something to be curious about, to engage with, to bring together into a team, where the team became well-rounded precisely because each human within it wasn't.

These insights, and the picture of work that they paint, have informed all of my work since. If work will always be a part of our lives—and, notwithstanding the more extreme predictions of an AI-saturated world, it will be—then we need methods and insights that ensure work works for us humans, and that find common ground between the goals of the organization and the yearnings of the person. These great managers showed us this common ground and, in doing so, launched a revolution in how the world of work viewed the strengths of each person. Today it's become conventional wisdom that the best managers focus on strengths and manage around weaknesses, and almost thirty million people have taken the two strengths assessments I helped create: StrengthsFinder and StandOut.

But today is also, in so many ways, a different day.

Although some of these original findings remain true—that people grow most in their areas of greatest strength and that the best managers treat each person differently and stay close to their people—the world we live in is clearly not the same. The digital revolution, the explosion and intrusion of social media, the pandemic, the proliferation of employee behavior-tracking software, advanced robotics, and now the onslaught of AI—all of it has utterly changed work, and our relationship to it.

Today your workplace reaches into your life far more deeply than twenty-five years ago. Your employer can not only see the personal opinions you express on social media, it can, and often does, police those opinions. The pandemic showed we could be just as productive working remotely, and yet many, if not all, corporate leaders didn't trust this finding—and so the current trend forces all employees back to the office, where devices track their entrances and exits, their keystrokes and choices at the vending machine, the number of their emails and the sentiments expressed in them, and even the movement of their pupils as they stare at, or, God forbid, look away from, their screens.

Our expectations as customers have changed too. We now demand immediate fulfillment of our desires, immediate delivery, see it/buy it/get it/return it, move on to the next desire. And of course, since everything is digital, our expectation for one class of products has become our expectation for all. If Amazon gives us a certain kind of online experience, that becomes our expectation for all kinds of online experience. "Best in class" or "industry leading" are now meaningless aspirations, since the best in one industry has upleveled our expectations across all industries.

Counterintuitively, as our expectations have risen our levels of trust have fallen. Back in the 1990s the team at Gallup was measuring how much trust people had in various organizations and institutions. The levels varied across the decades, but last year was the first year that no large organization—not government, not the armed forces, not schools, not media, not tech, not health care—had more than 15 percent of people expressing trust in them. Most of us feel we are moving through a world that isn't made for us. Yes, we can get what we want with one word to our phone, but no, we don't feel safe in our world. Everything is available to us, but nothing protects us. Nothing has our back. It is an abundant but amoral world. Efficient but unloving. It all works, but in many important ways, it is broken.

Faced with this world, what now must leaders do?

What mindsets, behaviors, and actions must they change in order to deserve the best people? What skills must they develop in order to deliver value to customers who are at once more demanding and more distrusting? How can leaders leverage AI and robotics to maximize efficiency, and yet still build deep reservoirs of goodwill and loyalty within employees and customers? What genuine things can they do to move people to productive action in an increasingly artificial world? Faced with shorter attention spans, little patience, and dwindling faith in one another, what can the best leaders do to rally people to a better future?

This book, a sequel twenty-five years in the making, addresses these questions.

Specifically, it will define the one hidden skill at the heart of all the best leaders today—and what you can do in your own working life to cultivate it.

Simply stated, the skill is this: *the deliberate design of the most powerful force in business.*

To bring it to life for you, and, I hope, give you guidance and inspiration for your own leadership, let me show you what this skill can look like in the real world. As you'll see, it's not beyond your reach. It's one of those skills that, while hard to master, is easy to start.

## Leading Lovingly

Stay with me. This isn't about kumbaya. But have you ever worked for someone who got the very best out of you? Someone you'd run through walls for? Someone who built the kind of team you desperately wanted to be on?

Maybe it was at school—your band leader, your sports team coach. Or maybe it was in the working world—it was a leader who attracted the best people and who lifted them up to extraordinary success. Everyone clamored to be on that team. People excelled on that team; people thrived. They were extremely productive but not burned out.

This leader delivered great results too, didn't they? It wasn't just all rah-rah, happy-happy, they also created great performances, won games, served customers, delivered amazing products and the best service, got things done. As if by magic, they made everyone feel alive—heart pounding, great work, daily progress, all of it.

I hope you come across a leader like this at some time in your life.

Josh is one such leader. He's a real person. I'll save for later what his real job is because revealing it now might prove distracting. For now, let me just share that, having worked his way up in the same company over the last three decades, he's now a very senior leader in a *Fortune* 100 company. It's the kind of company that affords its leaders significant status, some of whom become quite comfortable with this status, gliding untouched through the halls and meeting rooms with a posse of handlers.

As part of my ongoing primary qualitative research into the best leaders, I had heard about Josh. That he rejected the posse, instead making it a point to be extremely accessible to all his employees at all times. That he was passionate about all details of the employee experience, from reviewing the lighting in the bathrooms to being present for staff anniversaries. That he was equally intense in his focus on his customers' experience, spending as many hours debating the correct color and location of trash cans as he would designing the newest, highest-tech entertainment spaces. That he was so fixated on experience-design that he had renamed his entire part of the company "__________ Experiences" to reinforce to both employees and customers that more than hospitality, or service, or even entertainment, they were first and foremost an experience company.

And though I hadn't met Josh personally, I had encountered firsthand what his colleagues called "The Josh Effect": while visiting his facilities a couple of months earlier with his head of people, we'd been let through by a security guard who asked about our business that day. Upon hearing that we were studying employee and customer experiences, the guard, unprompted, launched into a detailed description of the conversation he and Josh had had the last time Josh came through his gate. Apparently Josh had remembered that the guard's son had just been hired by the company, and so they had a fatherly catch-up about the joys and challenges of getting one's kids started on their journey of work.

"Love that guy," the guard said. "He's one of the good ones."

Whenever I hear, and see, examples of extreme positives, my curiosity kicks in. Is it real? What does the leader actually do? What disciplines do they stick to no matter what? So I asked to interview Josh and spend a day-in-the-life with him at work.

It was, I must say, the most extraordinary day of research I have ever spent. Over the years, I've conducted many day-in-the-life studies, and indeed, many with Josh's peers at his company. Never have I seen what I witnessed with him.

The day began with the two of us chatting for a few minutes in a break room, with the plan being that he would then walk me through the facility and highlight which touchpoints of the employee or customer experience he paid attention to, and which actions he then took.

The plan fell apart before it began.

While I was in the restroom, he disappeared. Finding him gone, I left the break room, knocking on doors and scouring the corridors, until someone poked their head out of a doorway and said: "Oh, Josh is this way. He's found a tour group."

A tour group?

I rounded the corner to find Josh standing outside in front of a small group of customers who'd paid to be given a special tour of the facility. Meeting someone as senior as Josh was most definitely not on the official tour agenda, but he had bumped into them and decided to hang out for a while and share what new developments he was most excited about and what they should look out for on their tour. He spent twenty minutes chatting with them, and, as he was eventually pulled away from the group, he made sure to shake every customer's hand and thank them for coming.

I was intrigued, scribbling away on my pad, but I also retained a clinical eye. He knew I was there. Perhaps this had an element of "show."

Then, as we met up and walked toward the public areas of the facility, an older gentleman approached him: "Hey Josh, great to see you! You know it's my fortieth anniversary with the company today! Would you mind taking a picture with me?"

Click, click, the picture taken, Josh then spots a cook whom he seems to know walking toward one of the employee entrances: "Hey!" Josh calls out. The cook turns, smiles, walks over, hugs, and they catch up for a while. It's an easy vibe. They may be chasms apart in company hierarchy, but the feeling is two friends happy to see each other.

From there, we walk through the door separating the employee-only areas from the customers, and we start to cross from one side of the property to the other. I'm anticipating it will take twenty minutes or so, as I look through his eyes and try to learn what grabs his attention, and why.

But the first twenty yards takes twenty minutes, and we never make it across the property. Because every few yards Josh is stopped by a customer. "Thank you," they tell him. "Can we get a picture?"

"Love what you're doing!"

"Great day!"

"Keep it up, Josh!"

"Can we get one too? Would you mind?"

I've never seen anything like it. My first thought is, *How do they even know who he is?* And then, quickly, my mind moves to: *Why are they thanking him? Why do they love him so much? If this is all for show, how did he get so many hundreds of customers to show up on cue?!*

And of course, this wasn't all for show. This mobbing—it's the only word for it—of Josh wasn't choreographed for my benefit. It was a product of countless previous decisions that he must have made over the preceding few years.

Decisions about how to think about his employees. How to talk with these employees. How to remember their names, listen to their concerns, act on their interests. And then these employee-focused decisions must have spilled over into connections to the customers. All of which he seemed to love. He wasn't stressed by the mobbing. On the contrary, he leaned into it, stopping for each person, each family group, asking about their day, thanking them for coming, smiling, talking, crouching down for the kids, hugging the moms and dads.

In between the selfies and the walking group shots, I manage to squeeze in my question: "How do they know who you are?"

"Not sure," he says. "I think it might be the Instagram account I set up for our employees. I wanted to show them that I was listening to their issues and ideas right now, today, and so I set up a public account for all employees to ask whatever they wanted. I was told this was risky—who knows what people will ask about—but I was fine with it. Let them ask! And let the customers see it!"

And so they did—ask and see. And the employees loved it. And clearly the customers did too. Here was a leader bucking the trend of desiccated, distrustful, surveillance-infected workplaces. Here was a leader betting on trust, and leading with love. In small ways—remembering names, honoring anniversaries, taking pictures—and large—creating "risky" public platforms to show employees how close and connected he was to their concerns.

I'm not a cynical person, but I am skeptical—a slightly uptight British researcher. What I saw that day cut through any psychometric skepticism. I saw lots of love that day. The customers were so thrilled to see him, beaming and laughing, and dashing back and forth to take pictures and get in one of them. And the employees—well, they were beaming too. And, I think the word is *proud*. Yes, they were proud to see him so beloved. Proud to be a part of that love. Proud that their leader was so obviously present and listening, a living, breathing human, there he was, standing there, standing for everything the customers wanted the company to stand for.

Other words I scribbled down that day: "uplifting," "connected," "as one," "coherent," "everyone leaning in," "He's not a celebrity, they love him because he's what they imagine a leader of this company to be." "They don't love him—they love that it's all true." "They love their own feelings." "Relief—we're not being tricked." "It's real."

This was more than a leader simply being friendly or caring. This was a leader deliberately designing love in to all his actions and decisions. Some of them went unseen by the masses: earlier in the day, and unbeknownst to Josh, I'd seen him spend thirty minutes on his haunches with a twelve-year-old girl who'd been granted a wish to spend a day on the property. Some of them were very public: at a staff celebration event where Josh was on live TV ringing the opening bell of the New York Stock Exchange, his words were all directed toward thanking the customers and reaffirming his and his team's commitment to serving them. The private, quiet words with the twelve-year-old, the public commitment to service, the hugs, the remembered names, the quick chats and catch-ups, these were all parts of a through line of genuine intent, of seeing and honoring each human, of love.

"Ours is a delicate, sensitive brand," Josh tells me later. "It lives in people's hearts. I'm just trying in everything I do to honor their heart."

It was a lovely day. In a world of separation and conflict, a frenetic, stressful, and distrusting world, here was an example of how one leader can change the experience of tens of thousands. One leader who refuses to accept the inevitability of lovelessness. One leader whose calculation is not *What can we get away with?* but instead who asks himself *What can we do to make each human feel genuinely seen?*

To all this, you might say: *Well, that's just who he is!*

And yes, for sure, as all great leaders do, Josh possesses some natural talent to connect. And a genuine desire to. But he also has a method. A clear set of beliefs, intentions, and actions. Which, over time, have become a discipline. And it's this discipline that, over time, has created genuine love in the hearts of employees and customers alike. He knows, as all excellent leaders do, that this love doesn't come about by accident. That if you want to be one of those leaders whom people say they love working for, they'd walk through walls for, you have to design it in to the way you lead.

Just as if you want your customers to say they love your product, or your service, or your brand, you have to design it in.

Josh designs it into all he does. He is *an experience-maker who has mastered the deliberate design of the most powerful force in business.*

My goal for this book is to teach you this skill to Design Love In—what I call DLI. Not so that you can become Josh; he's a unique leader, as are you. But so that you can find your way of mastering the same skill he has. And so, in your own unique way, create the same extremely positive outcomes as he has.

## Leaders Are Experience-Makers

Many leaders begin with an assumption about human behavior that feels intuitively correct but turns out to be inaccurate. They believe people encounter a situation, interpret it, think through a set of options, weigh the consequences, and then choose the behavior that seems most reasonable. It's a clean, appealing model of how humans operate: stimulus, cognition, decision, action.

To watch humans in a real-life environment, however, is to see something entirely different. In workplaces of every kind—in clinics, factories, stores, corporate offices, classrooms, and call centers—we humans, whether employees or customers, do not pause and reflect. We react. To the cues of the environment and the people within it. A patient asks a question, and the nurse moves toward the bed before they have consciously thought through their response. A team member expresses concern in a meeting, and the leader instinctively slows down their voice. A bored associate looks away from a customer, and instinctively the customer leans out and begins to walk away.

What is actually occurring inside us humans is a rapid interplay of forces—emotional, sensory, perceptual, physiological—each pushing or pulling us in a particular direction. These forces aren't random. They are triggered by the experiences we're having. Each touchpoint in an environment—the too-bright lighting in that ice cream parlor, the clinical tone of that onboarding email from the recruiter, the cold voice of the AI agent on the customer service line—is raw material. We see it, hear it, feel it, sense it. We "pick up" what's been "put down" in the environment, and from all of it we shape an experience. An experience that lives within us, that we carry around with us, and that shapes our next action, and our next. Our experiences—owned by us, created by us, carried by us—contain the forces that shape our behavior. Forces far more powerful than deliberate decision-making.

You've felt this, haven't you? You've found yourself hurrying out of a grocery store because something about the clutter of pallets and the barrage of pricing signs set you on edge. You've lingered longer in a restaurant because you sensed the rapport among the waitstaff. You might not have been able to pinpoint which glance or which gesture created your experience, but instinctively it felt warm and welcoming, and you wanted to stay. And at work, you've come to realize that you're prepared to strive harder for this team than for any other, and it's not one thing but all the things, weaving themselves into the fabric of an experience, that reinforce your feeling that yes, this team has my back.

Our experiences shape our behavior, which shapes our outcomes. This is the deep logic of leadership.

Yet most leadership practices attempt to shape behavior directly. Leaders are told to issue directives, set goals, and offer feedback, coaching, recognition, and corrections—and to do the same for customers, by defining prices, offering incentives, and establishing service levels. All of these are useful tools, but none of them reach the internal forces that drive behavior. They address the surface but not the source.

For leaders to create reliable, repeatable changes in behavior, they must focus on the experience that creates the forces that create the behavior. This means leaders must understand their real job. Leadership is not fundamentally about clarifying expectations or motivating teams or cascading strategies. Leadership is the craft of shaping the experiences that shape human behavior. Leaders—the most effective ones—are experience-makers.

This insight reframes leadership entirely. Every moment between a leader and a colleague or a leader and a customer is an experience. The first day on the job is an experience. The weekly check-in is an experience. Sending an email is an experience. Presenting work is an experience. Being recognized, being challenged, being supported—or conversely, being dismissed or ignored—are all experiences. What we measure on employee and customer surveys are felt experiences. What we label "culture" is really just the aggregated experiences of the employees. When we say we want to build a strong culture, what we actually mean is that we want to design every touchpoint so carefully that each person has a similar experience. (And culture building is so hard precisely because there are so many touchpoints that have to be designed.)

Always remember that because leaders create experiences in every moment, they are *always* shaping the internal forces that shape behavior. The question is not whether you, as a leader, are an experience-maker. You are. The question is whether you're a skilled one.

So to help you build this skill, in part one of the book you'll learn that love isn't purely mysterious—that instead, love, when deconstructed, reveals itself to comprise *five distinct feelings*. These five feelings are sequential. You start with number one and end with number five. The leader with the DLI skill knows how to use this sequence as their blueprint for designing love in to anything—from onboarding to a team meeting to a customer interaction to a brand.

You'll discover the *one lens* through which to look at the world. A lens that spotlights where the most powerful possibilities lie, and how to maximize them. Most leaders go a lifetime without looking through this lens, and so miss the levers, the sources of power the world is offering them. Here in this book, you'll learn how to wear this lens, how to see the world radically differently and, I hope, never take it off.

You'll learn about something called the *experience continuum*, which shows you why the world you live in—and that your team and customers live in—feels so stressful and frustrating, and so physically and psychologically depleting. The experience continuum will show you how to unpack all of this and make sense of it, and, crucially, it will show you what you can do to transform our loveless world into something far better.

In part two of the book, you'll take these insights, this data and these perspectives, and put them into practice. Specifically, you'll learn the playbook for how to design love in to the experiences of those you lead and of those you serve.

The two roles leaders play in doing this are Mover and Maker. Mover focuses on the leader's ability to design love in to their own work. They know that health isn't balance. Health is motion. And so, they're deliberate about how they move through all the parts of their life, and the days of their life, and draw the energy they need to keep moving. My previous book, *Love + Work*, taught the techniques of this Mover role.

Where Mover targets your own experiences, Maker addresses the experiences of others. You, the DLI leader, can make experiences for others, and those experiences then affect what they do. When played well, this role sees you at your most inspirational and influential.

How to excel at the Maker role is the focus of part two of this book.

You might think that experience-making is not your job. It's marketing's job. Or those folks over in brand. Or human resources. Or it's digital's job as they plot out various website "customer journeys" or "employee experience life cycles." And sure, marketing, brand, HR, and digital all have their part to play in creating the kinds of experiences that people love. But, in reality, all they are doing—at their best—is laying the foundations for generally good experiences for customers or employees. The brand folks can make vivid promises. The marketing folks can write clear and compelling calls to action. The HR and digital teams can design their screens using the most up-to-date, human-centric, user-experience design principles.

But none of these are what creates extreme positive experiences. A person's true experience working on your team will include how you speak to them, how the break room looks to them, the tone of that email, the expressions of their colleagues as they greet them in the morning and say goodbye when they leave.

And yes, the experience of your customer might begin with brand, price, and product, but it builds and builds through the words of the customer service person, the smell of the store or product, the message played to them while on hold, the look and feel of the chairs in the waiting room, the location of the trash cans—all of it combines to create an experience, one that affects what this customer chooses to do next.

And all of these parts of the experience are within your control.

The DLI leader doesn't outsource experience-design to other departments. Instead, they know that, no matter how much good design work might have been done by the brand, marketing, human resources, or digital teams, the reality of what working on this team is actually like, or what shopping in this store or being a client of this service is actually like—all of this lies in the hands of you, the local leader.

Other departments make the promises. It's you, the local leader of the local team, who keeps them.

Stepping skillfully into the Maker role explains why leaders such as Josh are so effective at attracting the most talented team members, and why, despite the temptations of an increasingly tight labor market, these team members stay. It explains why they excel at stitching a fabric of connections with customers, who then return more often, stay longer, spend more, and spread the word to friends and family. This skill is the source of high performance, but also resilience. Of productivity, but also creativity. Of physical and also mental health. It's the foundation for all good things today, and it's the mechanism through which these leaders will create a better future tomorrow.

And if we raise our sights beyond countable business outcomes, this skill has the power to change the moral trajectory of our world. We will get more of what we accept, and increasingly we are finding it acceptable to live in a transactional world where classrooms are fixated on the grades of the student, not their talents and dreams; where employees are labeled "headcount" rather than actual people; where our attention online is measured, mined, and monetized; where our illnesses are evaluated first by how much of them are "covered"; where all of us—students, employees, patients, and customers—are understood primarily as elements in an equation, all parts of us weighed, rationalized, assessed, and maximized against return-on-investment calculations.

This skill—embodied in leaders like you—can save us from this dispiriting world, where everything functions but nothing flourishes. It can show us that the current trajectory of our world is unacceptable. That in order to have a life that works, we do not have to sacrifice what makes life worth living. This skill can help you do what all great leaders do: lift us above our current predicament and step up to something far better.

The employee on his fortieth anniversary was so happy to have found Josh to celebrate with. The cook leaned into Josh, his friend and colleague, and shared a laugh. The customers flocked to Josh because in him they warmed to a person who was there for them, who felt what they were feeling, who seemed to want to slow down and listen to their thanks, their excitement, their glee. They were all drawn to the real-life-ness of one leader paying attention. Spending a minute, or thirty minutes, one leader bothering to honor the delicate, seemingly fleeting feelings of love. Feelings that, these days, we all miss—and we all crave.

Yes, this DLI skill will lead you in surprising, and for some, disorienting, directions. But I hope you keep your mind and your heart open to it. It might just change your life and show you how to build a bigger one—for yourself, for those you lead, and for those you serve.

## Is Yours a DLI Company?

Finally, at the end of the book we'll define the nonnegotiables for a DLI company.

The opposite of design is drift. When we look away from love, when we unchain ourselves from the most powerful force in business, we lose our frames of reference. We can't tell the difference between a shortcut and a distraction, smart and stupid, value building and value breaking, we lose our focus, up is down, down is up, unchained and unmoored, we drift.

This is where so many companies and leaders find themselves today.

To make meaningful change, you, the DLI leader, can do your part in building a DLI company. A company that puts love at the center of all they do—not to be soft, but instead because love is the most powerful driver of extreme positive business outcomes. Currently we've lost our fluency in the language of love. At the most reputable business schools there are no classes on how to deconstruct business's most powerful force, nor on how you, the leader, can channel this force for productive ends. It's absurd when you think about it. This force, properly marshaled, creates everything good a business wants—and yet we're virtually blind to it.

In the years to come I'm going to do everything I can to change this failing. Specifically, my focus will be to educate as broadly as possible the millions of folks who've taken my strengths assessments that the only places deserving of their strengths are DLI companies. You have only this one life: Why devote your precious strengths to a loveless organization? Why work for a place that sees you as merely an element in a transaction, to be maximized and discarded at will? You wouldn't want yourself—or your kids—to work for a place like this, would you? No, me neither.

So, together let's commit ourselves to highlighting how unwise loveless companies are, the kind that operate efficiently and make their numbers each quarter by hiring, then laying off, large swaths of their workers; the kind that create spans of control so large that one supervisor has to manage sixty team members; the kind that treat their customers like hostages and their employees like headcount.

These companies are unworthy of you. They are ubiquitous, but uninspiring. Let's define what a DLI company looks like, how it operates, what its nonnegotiables are—and then, together, as a unified voice, let's teach as many talented workers as possible that a loving organization is the only one they should accept.

Let's set up DLI as the gold standard. And let the others drift away into mediocrity.

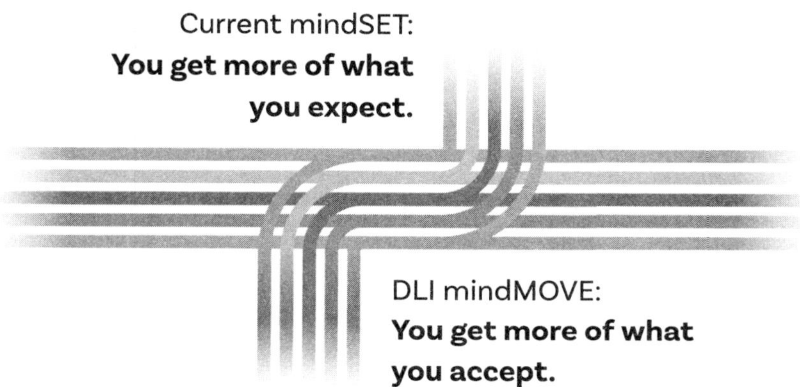

## Part One

# LOVE DECONSTRUCTED

# 1

# Experiences Drive Behaviors Drive Outcomes

I understand you may be skeptical about love as the most powerful force in business. So, for your foundation, look past matters of the heart, put aside the images of delighted customers and workers bursting with pride, and instead, dive into a bit of data. You're a business leader. You live in a world of metrics, and scorecards, and careful calculations of ROI. So, yes, start with data.

What precisely is the business case for love?

## The Business Case for Love

As a leader, you know what you want. You want outcomes.

You want high performance from your people. You want retention. You want your customers to buy more, stay longer, and feel strong personal loyalty to your business.

And you know that these outcomes aren't magicked into existence. That, instead, these outcomes are created by certain repeated behaviors. For your people to perform, they will need to plan their time well, prioritize the right things, put in the hours, collaborate with each other, and give you every ounce of "discretionary effort." For your customers to become loyal, they will have to choose to return more frequently, to buy more, and to voluntarily advocate for your company to friends and family.

And on some level, you know that you can't force either employees or customers to display these behaviors. You know that a person's productive behaviors, such as working harder, or spreading positive word of mouth, are a choice the person makes, and that what causes these choices are the person's experiences. If your team members have extremely positive experiences working on your team, they are more likely to display extremely positive behaviors, and so create extremely positive outcomes. The same applies to your customers: you know that if they've had great experiences, those experiences will impact their behaviors, which in turn will produce the outcomes you want.

Intuitively you understand this sequence: experiences drive behaviors drive outcomes. Want the best outcomes? Design the best experiences.

Intuitions can be wise, but still, as business professionals, it's always comforting to see the data. Back in 1994 James Heskett, Earl Sasser, and Leonard Schlesinger introduced us to the service-profit chain, which posited a strong causal link between employee experiences leading to customer experiences, leading to customer loyalty, leading to profitability. A couple of years later Joseph Pine and James Gilmore proposed that we were entering what they called the experience economy—the latest step in a progression from agrarian, to industrial, to service, to digital, to the experience economy. And that in this experience economy the thriving companies would be those that created deeply immersive experiences for customers. Starbucks, they told us, doesn't sell coffee; they sell a coffee-house experience, a third place, when we tire of work and home. Disney parks don't sell rides; they sell a trip to fantasy lands, which just happen to have rides within them. Apple doesn't sell phones in their stores; instead they immerse us in a world that showcases and embodies Apple's love of design.

The service-profit chain and the experience economy were theories, offered up to help us understand how the world works. I'm happy to report that a close review of the data across many thousands of studies, across many decades, confirms the validity of these theories. If you want extreme positive outcomes, you need to create extreme positive experiences. Because experiences drive behaviors drive outcomes.

The graphs in these studies tend to look like the one in figure 1-1. This one happens to be a retailer in the United States with just over eight thousand stores. Each store has approximately one hundred employees, and thousands of customers. When you measure the employee and customer experiences through a simple survey, where 1 is

**FIGURE 1-1**

**Relationship of customer and employee experiences to store profitability**

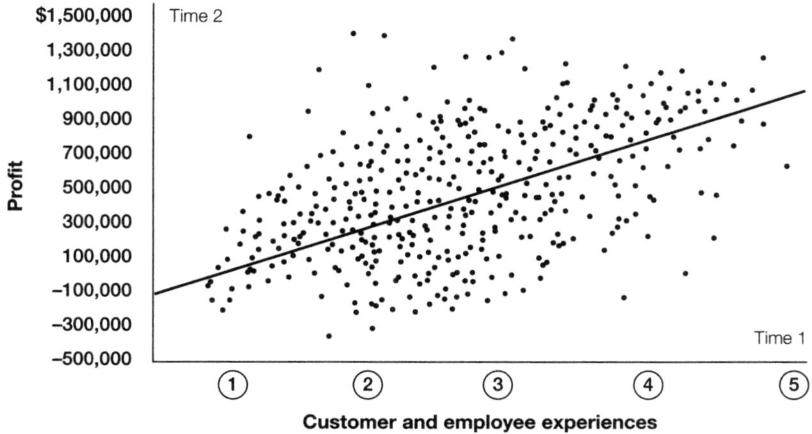


*Source*: The Buckingham Institute.

strongly negative and 5 is strongly positive, and you plot each store's experiences against each store's profitability, you get this graph.

The black dots are stores, and as you can see from the line going from bottom left to top right, in general the stores that delivered better measured experiences for customers and employees produced higher levels of profitability. The link isn't perfect—you can see a few stores far above and far below the line of best fit—but overall, the pattern in this company is quite clear. Those stores that created positive experiences created positive outcomes.

The challenge for the executives of this company, of course, is that not all of the stores are creating the same kinds of experiences. Yes, this company selects and trains and pays and promotes its people in the same way: it supposedly has one company culture. And yes, each store offers their customers very similar merchandise presented on very similar shelves in very similar aisles. And yet, as you can see, there's quite a range in actual experiences being felt by both employees and customers. Figure 1-2 is identical to figure 1-1 except for the addition of arrows pointing to certain stores, and, as the arrows highlight, for every store that's delivering extreme positive experiences like the one at the top right of the figure, there are plenty of others delivering something quite different.

No executive wants to see this kind of variation. Yes, the trend line looks nice and consistent, but double-click into the detail of this company and what you see is range. While this company may have one stock price, and while it may present to the world one uniform company culture—defined and celebrated on websites and handbooks and break room walls—the real-world experiences of employees and customers vary wildly.

This graph isn't an anomaly. Take virtually any organization's employee or customer experience survey data, and slice it by team or department or, as in this case, by store, and what you see is variation between one team and another, inside the same company. No one likes to talk about this much because the motive of leaders at the

FIGURE 1-2

**Variability in customer and employee experiences**

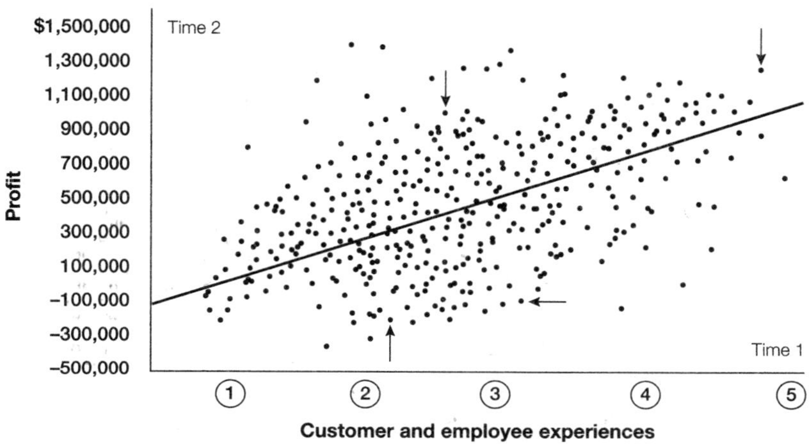


*Source:* The Buckingham Institute.

executive committee level is to project an aura of control, as in *We know how our business runs, and we are in control of the various levers we need to pull in order to net the outcomes we want.*

But in the real world, the data measuring customer and employee experiences has high standard deviations inside the same organization. High standard deviations mean a lack of control. While the executives may want to be able to control how people experience their company, the reality is that how a person experiences the company—whether as a customer or an employee—varies significantly by which store they happen to work in or shop at.

If experiences are the building blocks of company culture, then, for most companies, these building blocks are higgledy-piggeldy. The experiences they are creating for employees and customers are undesigned. And, as you can see so clearly from figure 1-2, this is a problem: undesigned experiences lead to unpredictable outcomes.

. . .

Here, let's pause briefly to draw a distinction between experiences, moments, and touchpoints.

An experience is owned by the person. It's what they feel inside, what they carry around with them, and what drives their behavior.

A moment is a chunk of an experience. Your experience of a drive-through restaurant is created from chunks of temporal moments—reading the menu is a moment, as is placing your order, as is paying, as is receiving your food. A moment isn't owned; it's shared between the designer/deliverer of the moment and the person receiving it.

A moment is defined as *a single interaction, prompting an immediate reaction.* Positive moments are great, but by themselves they have little impact on a person's behavior. If the host remembers your name or the certain kind of table you like, that's wonderful. If you get an encouraging note from a mentor, or a quiet word from your boss ("Great job, the team really counts on you!"), or a call from your mom, or a smile and an *After you!* wave from a fellow motorist, these are moments—they are unexpected, surprising, and, when good ones happen, they can turn your mood around. They're like vitamin $B_{12}$ shots, giving you a little boost for the rest of your day.

But they won't affect your behavior until you have a series of them. You see, the difference between a moment and an experience lies in the word *prediction.* An experience is defined as a *series of moments affecting memory, meaning, emotion, and action.* The unique power of an experience is that the person has internalized this series of moments: they've registered them again and again to such an extent that they can now *predict* that they'll experience them again and again. That if they go back to that store, they can predict that they will be recognized by the staff and called by name—it happened last week, and this week, and it'll happen again next week. That if they work hard for the team, they can predict that they will be called out and praised in the next team huddle—it happened last week, and this week, and they know that if they perform well next week, it'll happen again.

Research by behavioral economists Daniel Kahneman and Barbara Fredrickson has suggested that what defines a person's memory of an experience are the peaks—the most extreme positive moments—and the ends—if it begins poorly but ends well, people tend to remember it well. This has come to be called the peak-end rule, and their research does seem to suggest that the peak and the end moments have outsize impact on the memory of the experience.

What's missing from their data, however, is prediction. Moments are real. And positive moments are good. And peak-end moments are important. But any one moment, even a peak-end one, doesn't greatly affect what any person does next. A moment jolts. It might even surprise and delight. But only experiences shape behavior. Only experiences evoke a prediction. Only when the person has experienced a series of moments again and again, and has internalized this series to such an extent that they can confidently predict them, only then does this affect their behavior and then their outcomes. It's only when they know for sure what a certain behavior will make them feel that the experience will drive them to behave in that way again—by returning to that store, or working harder for that team.

The final pieces of the experience puzzle are touchpoints. Touchpoints are the raw material of experiences, the building blocks from which experiences are made. Yes, each moment is a touchpoint—but so are many other parts of the experience. They are *any sensory element of an experience perceived by the person.* Some touchpoints are sounds—the volume and style of the hold music is part of your experience as you wait in line for your representative, as is the tone of their voice when they finally pick up, and whether or not they use or remember your name. Some are sights—lying flat in the chair at the dentist, the sight of stained ceiling tiles intrudes into your experience and starts you questioning your dentist's passion for cleanliness. And some touchpoints are literally what you touch—the gray plastic seat cushions sticking to the backs of your bare legs in the DMV waiting room reinforce your sense that this entire experience wasn't designed with your comfort in mind.

We humans are experience-makers. Our reticular activating center registers each sensory touchpoint of an experience, we pick up what's put down in front of us, and instinctively we weave these touchpoints into an experience—a *story* we tell ourselves about how this experience makes us feel now, and a *prediction* about how it will make us feel if we experience it again.

This means that experiences—those things that actually drive human behavior—have to be designed, one touchpoint after another, in a carefully crafted series. A recruiting experience, for example, is made up of a series of touchpoints. The content of your recruitment ad is a touchpoint. The content of the emails you (or your applicant tracking system) send out is a touchpoint. The tone of the emails is a touchpoint. As are the images on the website, and the application form you ask your candidates to complete. As are the interview questions you use in your selection process, and where these interviews take place. As are your acceptance notifications, and your rejections. Each of these touchpoints combines, either haphazardly or intentionally, to create an experience in the heart of each candidate, and this experience is what they carry around with them, and what then drives their behavior.

So, while thinking about which moments matter is not a bad use of your time, it is not as powerful as thinking about how to design experiences using a series of sensory touchpoints that build on one another, over time. Because to create extreme positive outcomes requires the design of—and, at the executive committee level, the scaling of—extreme positive experiences.

Throughout the rest of the book, we'll explore how you, the DLI leader, can master the skill of using touchpoints to design experiences.

But before we do, let's examine precisely what kind of experiences the best leaders design.

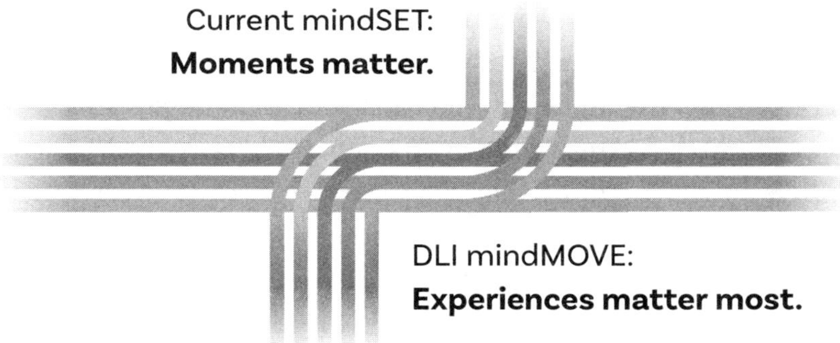


## Only 5s Are Predictive

Given how effective the very best leaders are at designing extreme positive experiences and generating the extreme positive outcomes the organization desires, you would have thought we would spend some meaty brain time studying those leaders.

Going back to that scatterplot graph in figures 1-1 and 1-2, this means that we would focus our attention on the leader of that team in the top right, and try to learn what precisely they were doing to create such positive experiences. And outcomes.

Strangely, that's not what most of us do.

Some part of our ignoring of positive experiences stems from what's called negativity bias. Rather than asking ourselves *Why did I feel so good yesterday? What happened that I could make happen again?* we look past these positives because they can't hurt us. Instead, we are acutely sensitive to what could go wrong in our lives, what situations or circumstances we need to avoid, and remain constantly on guard against them. We see this negativity in our work lives as well—when our manager insists that our route to success is to fix our failings, or when the big bosses highlight all the red numbers on the scorecard.

It's as if many of us live in a 1–3 world, where our fixation is on the 1s in figure 1-3, on what's going wrong, and how we can move them to a 3, the average. The parent who focuses primarily on their child's F grade, the manager who calls your weaknesses your "areas of opportunity" and tells you to work on fixing them, the leader who highlights the struggling teams and prioritizes resources to move them from struggling to surviving, from below average to average, these are all denizens of a 1–3 world.

Where we should be living, of course, is in a 1–3–5 world. In this world, while we can't ignore the 1s, we know that failure in something, a 1, doesn't teach us much about excellence in that thing, a 5. We know that studying divorce doesn't reveal the secrets of happy marriage, that fixing mistakes for a customer, while welcome, doesn't explain the true sources of deep-seated customer loyalty, and that

**FIGURE 1-3**

**The 1–3 world**

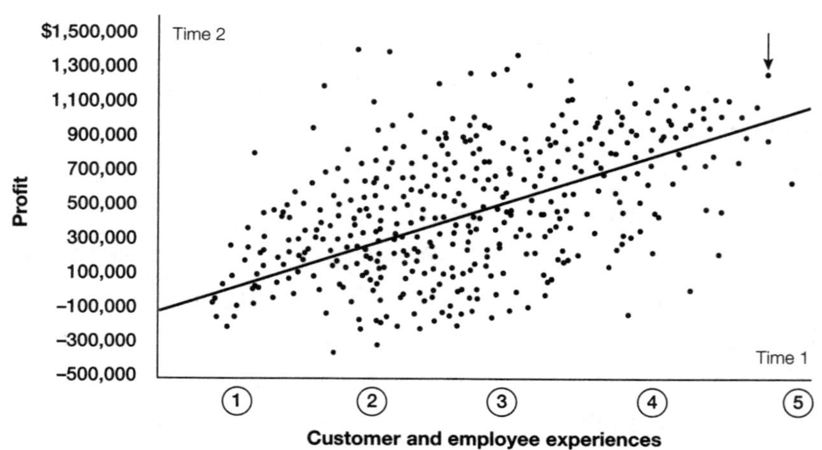


*Source*: The Buckingham Institute.

doing exit interviews with employees who leave tells us little about how to get others to stay. In a 1–3–5 world, we know that excellence isn't the opposite of failure; it's just different. And that to understand the ingredients of excellence, we must study the 5s.

Leaders locked into a 1–3 world make a second critical error. Fearful of the negative pull of the 1s, they don't investigate the 5s because they don't think it's worth it. There's no ROI in the 5s, they tell themselves. The 5s are as good as they're going to be. They are outliers. Weird exceptions, happy accidents, black swans.

Instead, these leaders say, let's invest our time in studying those experiences that are below average and try to move them to average, and then try to move the average ones to above average.

That, at any rate, is what this company asked of me. It looked at the large number of stores clustered in the left and middle of the range, and asked me to investigate those stores where customers and employees were rating their experience a 1, 2, or 3. Their reasoning was that because of the large number of stores clustered on the left and in the middle, if they could move the below-average stores to average, and the average stores to above-average, then, in aggregate, the overall profitability of the company would increase the most.

On the surface this seemed sensible. But in reality, they were making an analytical error. They were assuming that, when it came to experiences driving behaviors driving outcomes, the world worked in a linear way, as in the graph shown in figure 1-4.

They assumed that if they moved the 1s to 2s, 2s to 3s, and 3s to 4s, they would get the same amount of outcomes' increase as if they moved the 4s to 5s—and so, since they had far more stores delivering 1, 2, and 3 experiences, they concluded that shifting them all one notch to the right was the best investment of their time and money.

This linear thinking is why you will so often see companies lumping the 4s and the 5s together and labeling them "top two box" or "percent favorable." The business goal thus becomes: the more people we can move into the "percent favorable" category of experience, the better outcomes we'll get.

FIGURE 1-4

**Linear progression from 1–5**

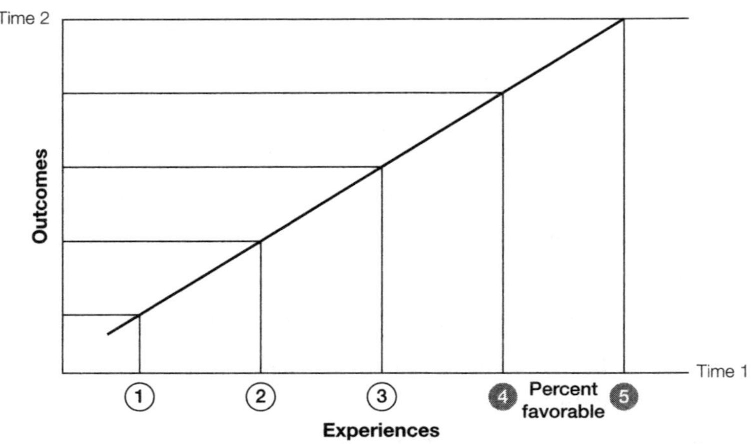


*Source:* The Buckingham Institute.

The problem with this assumption is that it's false. When it comes to experiences driving behaviors driving outcomes, the world does not work in a linear fashion. I know that the black dot scatterplot graph of figures 1-1, 1-2, and 1-3 looks as though it works linearly—that line of best fit moves straight from bottom left to top right. But I have to tell you that if you combine hundreds of scatterplot graphs such as that one, hundreds of studies examining the link between experiences at Time 1 and outcomes at Time 2, this line doesn't stay straight. As you add study after study, the line begins to curve, and curves more and more, until you discover that, when it comes to experiences driving behaviors driving outcomes, the real world works in a curvilinear fashion. (To review the research paper detailing the curvilinear relationship between experiences and outcomes, please visit DesignLoveIn.com.)

To give you a sense of what *curvilinear* looks like, figure 1-5 shows the links between seven sorts of experiences—confidence on the part of investors, and satisfaction on the part of students, employees, patients, and customers—and then the outcomes of

**FIGURE 1-5**

**The relationship of experiences to outcomes**

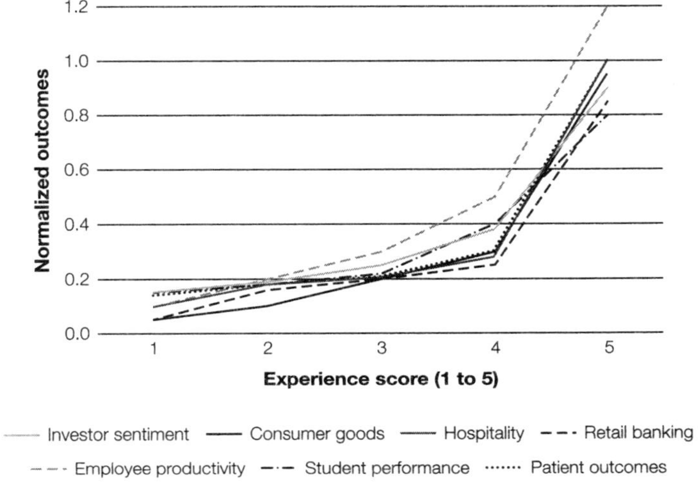


*Source:* The Buckingham Institute.

these experiences: financial return for the investors, health outcomes for the patients, grade achievement for the students, productivity for the employees, and return visits/purchases for the customers.

When you combine graphs such as these with thousands of other "Time 1 experiences to Time 2 outcomes" research findings, you get a graph that looks like the one in figure 1-6.

What I hope you can see from that figure is that moving "below average" experiences (the 1s and 2s) to "average" (the 3s) doesn't lead to much increase in outcomes at all. Nor does moving the "average" (the 3s) to "above average" (the 4s).

It's only when you somehow manage to do something so extremely positive for employees or customers that they rate their experience a 5 that you see a dramatic change in their behavior, which in turn creates a dramatic increase in the outcomes you want: they are more loyal, more productive, spend more, are safer, and are more likely to advocate for the company as a place to work, or shop.

FIGURE 1-6

**Effect of extreme positives**

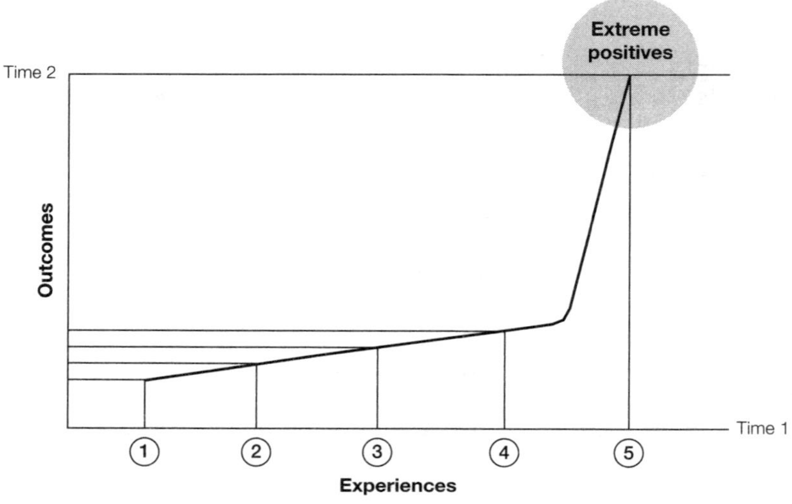


*Source:* The Buckingham Institute.

When it comes to experiences—yours, your team's, your students', your customers', your patients'—4s are not 5s.

The 4s are 3s. (One takeaway from this, if you value reliable data, is that you should never again combine 4s and 5s and label it "percent favorable" or "top two box." Combining 4s with 5s lumps two things together that are categorically different, thereby confusing you as to what's actually happening in the real world. Combining them might make the numbers larger, and therefore more palatable to present, but it ruins their validity.)

We should take the 5s seriously, and study the heck out of those extremely positive experiences not because it's more fun, or because we don't want to look at the negative. We should study the 5s because only then will we be able to know what kinds of extremely positive experiences drive extremely positive outcomes.

This is the key takeaway from the last twenty-five years of human experience data: Only "5" experiences predict outcomes.

You should see everything else—the 4s, the 3s, the 2s, and the 1s—as simply "not a 5."

This is true in your own life, as much as it is in business. Your 4s are those experiences where when someone asks you how it was, you find yourself saying, yeah, good, no complaints. That dinner, that book, that workday, that flight? Yeah, not bad at all. Fine.

While such experiences surely feel better than the 1s, in terms of driving your positive behavior they are indistinguishable.

Your 5s are the very things that make your life's journey worthwhile. Fives are those experiences you'll always say yes to. The ones you can't stop yourself from thinking about and looking forward to, even if you wanted to. Your 5s are your sources of energy that not only move you forward, but also color how your moving actually feels to you. Your 5s define your life, and your living.

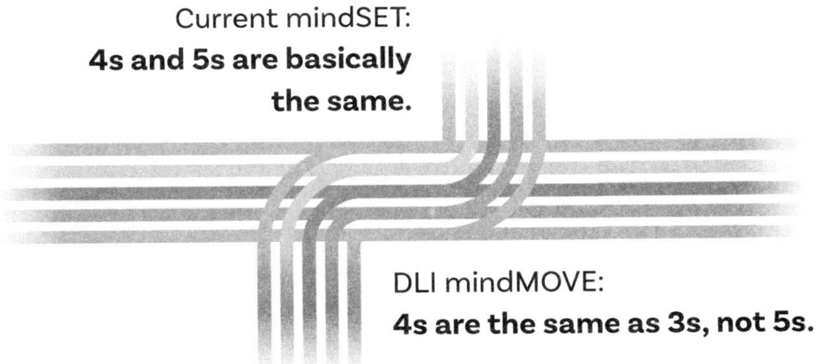


## What's in a 5?

I've spent the last three decades studying the 5s. Extreme positive human behavior has been my subject and my passion. I've interviewed thousands of people who were extraordinarily good at their job, trying to learn all I could about why they were so successful. I've done focus group after focus group with the most productive teams to try to figure out why they worked so well together. I've pored over the survey transcripts from hundreds of thousands of customers and patients, searching for what might have caused some of them to have such extremely positive experiences.

And all of them kept telling me. And I kept looking past it.

I'm not saying I didn't learn anything useful. The concept of employee engagement emerged from the study of great teams, and dissecting their ingredients and how to create them became the focus for my first book. The importance of capitalizing on your strengths was revealed in all the interviews with top performers, and the challenge of measuring a person's strengths accurately became the focus of those two assessments I and my colleagues created, StrengthsFinder and StandOut. The link between customer satisfaction and return visits, the hierarchy of customer loyalty, the demands of leadership—all of these emerged from my systematic study of the 5s.

What I'd missed was the force tying all these concepts together.

Well, in truth, I hadn't missed it. I'd heard it again and again—I just didn't believe it. It was too obvious. Not business-y enough. Not science-y enough.

As a psychometrician dedicated to finding reliable ways to measure human experiences, what I was supposed to do when studying the 5s was:

1. listen to the actual words that people use to describe their experiences;
2. believe those words; and then
3. put those words into the survey and assessment questions I was building to see whether they "worked"—that is, did they successfully measure a key aspect of the person's extremely positive experience or behavior?

I wasn't supposed to judge the words they used, or correct them, or make them sound "better." I was simply supposed to hear them, and then construct questions around them.

Shame on me, but over the years of studying 5s, I gradually stopped doing the work outlined in the list above. I came to think I knew a little bit more than those I was interviewing. I kept hearing the same word from the top-performing teams, the most loyal customers, and the most successful individuals, and rather than just running with the word they were using, I kept changing it. To *engagement*. Or *satisfaction*. Or *passion*. *Joy*. *Strengths*. *Talent*. *Resilience*. *Flow*. *Care*. The list got pretty long. And the problem wasn't that these words were necessarily wrong, or unhelpful, or misguided: the problem was that they hid the most powerful force of all.

Because the word these 5s kept using to describe their experiences was *love*.

A top salesperson: "What I love most about what I do is getting to the close!"

A heavy user (four times per month) of a particular restaurant: "I love that they know my favorite dessert."

A long-tenured employee: "I love this company. I can't imagine a world without it!"

A highly effective leader: "I love all my team. All of them. I'd do anything for them, and they know it."

This is what it sounded like. The unprompted use of an uncomplicated four-letter word.

Perhaps you can see why I kept reaching for something else, something more intellectual, more practical, more in sync with the corporate world. *Love* felt too soft, too emotive, lazy even, a careless exaggeration of the word *like*.

After the sale of my company, and the withering away I witnessed, a dam in my brain broke and I reapplied myself to studying the 5s. Every couple of years I put the surveys and the assessments aside and go out into the real world to do what's called primary qualitative research. I keep a running list of people and places that have been brought to my attention as examples of extreme positives, and I go interview them. Just ask open-ended questions and shut up and listen. Or, in the case of Josh, dodge through the delighted crowds and scribble as best I can.

During one of these interviews, with an environmental-engineer-turned-yoga-instructor named Jeanette, whose classes were so popular they were fully booked a year in advance, I got a crashing glimpse of the power of the obvious.

"Why are your classes so much more popular than anyone else's?" I asked. "You use the same studio, do the same routines, at roughly the same times as the other instructors. What's so different about your classes?"

We talked around and about a range of issues until all of a sudden, she paused, got up out of her chair, and said, "You know what I love?" She moved her body slowly and deliberately into what I came to learn was a pose called Warrior 2 (forgive me: I am no yoga expert). "What I love is finding this pose and then showing each of my students how to hold their hip here, in line with their left leg, even though every part of them wants that hip to roll and turn like this." She made what appeared to me to be an infinitesimally small adjustment to her hip. "See? How great is that! Each class, with each student, I get to do this. To show them the power of aligning the body. That it's here"—she moved her leg back a millimeter—"not here." As she does this, I see that though she's smiling her big broad smile, she is also crying.

And looking at her, with that inside-out glow of love for the tiniest detail of her work, for her service to her students, I saw all at once what these students must feel every single time they come to her class. To be in the presence of this love, something so pure, yet so technical, so of herself, yet so completely in service of them, was what drew them back time and again. This was why her classes were booked so far in advance: Once you'd felt this experience you didn't want to let it go. In a loveless world, you wanted to feel this love again and again.

Rereading the transcripts of the interviews and the focus groups, I found that this simple four-letter word was *always* there. I couldn't keep avoiding it—even though, with my formal British upbringing, I really wanted to. The fact pattern was so consistent and so compelling: Whenever a person's experiences were so positive they drove the most productive kinds of outcomes—high performance, creativity, resilience, loyalty—the word *love* was used. When the best experiences drive the best behaviors drive the best outcomes, those experiences are loving.

When top performers say they "love" some aspect of what they do, I immediately know a whole lot about them and their behavior. I know that they'll want to keep coming back to this activity and seeking out opportunities to do more of it. I know that when they're doing this thing they love, they'll work more fluently and feel less stress. I know that, measurably, they are much more likely to stay in this job and to advocate for their company as a place to work to friends and family.

The same applies to customers. Audience-testing data for movies reveals that the number of audience members saying "I really enjoyed that" or "I thought it was great" is largely irrelevant. Instead, the only metric that matters is how many spontaneous "I loved it!'s" you get. Because only once a person says "I loved it" can the studio be sure that this person will tell others to go see the movie, will talk it up in conversations and social posts, and even go back themselves to see it multiple times.

This is true for all customers of all products. It's only when you've managed to do something so compelling, so profound, so genuine, so moving that the customer says "I loved it!" that you're able to predict their subsequent behavior—such as repeat visits and purchases, voluntary advocacy to friends and family, or taking the initiative to look for more products and experiences from your company.

The same applies in schools. When a student says "I love my school" or "I love my teacher" the data shows they are far more likely to graduate.

I'm sure this fits with your own experience. You've had a great many teachers throughout the course of your life, and some of them were quite competent in transferring their knowledge to you. You respected them. You enjoyed some of their classes. But only a very few teachers, perhaps only one, reached you in such a profound way that now, looking back, you'd say *Yes, wow, I really loved that teacher.*

Everywhere I looked I saw that when people owned the word *love*, when they instinctively tied the "love" label to their feelings of an experience, it was related to them acting in all sorts of productive ways. In direct contrast, when they said "liking" or "really enjoying" or being "satisfied," it told me virtually nothing about a person's future behavior. The feeling of love was in a different category altogether, producing utterly different sets of behaviors.

When it comes to driving productive human behaviors, our feelings, the data suggests, are binary: there is love, and there is everything else. And everything else is simply "not love." It's as if our feelings have a boiling point, and unless they reach that point, they are nonpredictive in terms of driving our behavior. If you heat water from 0 degrees to 11 degrees Fahrenheit, it is not boiling. Heat it further to 111 degrees, and it is not boiling. Heat it all the way up to 211, and it is still not boiling. The only time when you can confidently predict that water will change its state from a liquid to a vapor is when it reaches 212 degrees (figure 1-7).

As with water, so with our feelings. When it comes to driving productive behaviors it's not just that love is more powerful than other feelings; it's that love is the *only* feeling that does so. If you say you like something, or enjoy it, or feel cared for, or respected, or joyful, or even passionate, while all of these are clearly in some sense "good" experiences for you, none of them helps me predict what you're going to do next. It's only when your experience reaches the "love" level that it starts to drive your behavior toward extreme positives.

Yes, of course, love, the feeling of being loved, of things being done to us lovingly, is the quintessence of the human experience. It's the

**FIGURE 1-7**

**Only love drives productive behaviors**

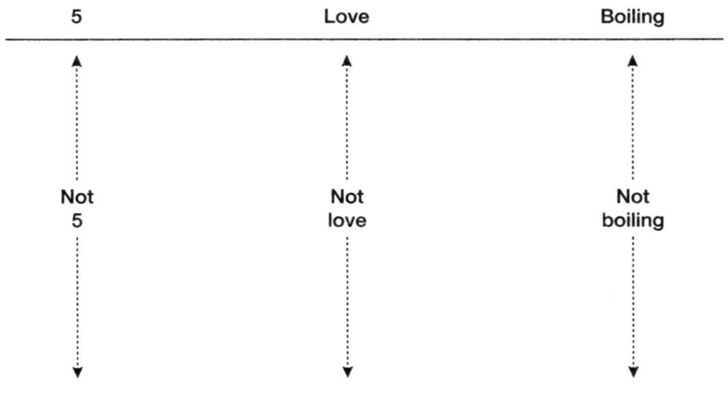


*Source:* The Buckingham Institute.

first human thing we reach for at our birth, the last we cling onto at our death, and is the source of our empathy for one another. But love is also *predictive.* It is the foundation of our loyalty to this brand, not that one, to this team, not that one. Our love of this specific activity, this certain moment, decodes the mystery of who we really are and guides us to contribute our best. Love fuels our resilience, sparks our creativity, and bonds us together as collaborators.

And love, in this context, doesn't mean chocolates and champagne and kissing in front of the Eiffel Tower. Nor does it mean simply caring for others. Love means passionate commitment to something or someone. Love means deep loyalty. Love is the driver of deliberate practice, the prime mover of discretionary effort. Love is advocacy. And, of course, love can be hard-edged, hence "tough love"—some of the toughest conversations you've ever had have been with people who loved you.

Yes, it can apply to weighty matters—"I love my work, I love my mentor!"—and to more modest ones—"I love this outfit!"; "I loved that movie!" But wherever and whenever we use the word *love,* extreme positive outcomes follow. There is no such thing as loveless excellence, loveless service, loveless creativity, loveless loyalty: wherever you find any of these things, you find love.

This is why the data shows: *Love is the most powerful force in business.* It's more a force than a feeling. A force for all things good.

Which makes it all the stranger that organizations don't have a strategy for it. They have a strategy for doing things efficiently, and cost-effectively, and, these days, artificially intelligently—but no strategy for doing things *lovingly.*

I was in a meeting in New York recently with thirty chief human resources officers of the largest companies in the world, and after I presented some of the data on love, they couldn't even say the word. After a little mental wrestling they became comfortable using it in reference to customers loving their product or their brand, but many still stumbled when applying it to their own people. Love is the most powerful driver of extreme positive outcomes, but we struggle to take it seriously. Not just in business, in our own lives as well. We have softened it and flattened it out into cliché. Love is a romantic dinner à deux. Love is *Love Island.* Or it's what we feel for our family. Or maybe, in the broadest sense, it's how we think about our career, as in *Find a job you love, and you'll never have to work again!*

But love as a specific force? Love as a category of experience worthy of study? Love as a definable resource? Love as something we could learn to design into our life, or the lives of those we lead and serve? No, that kind of love seems fanciful to us.

Let's change that. Let's spend our time together taking love seriously. Let's demystify love, reverse engineer it, if you will, and reveal its ingredients. Of course, the feeling of love will always retain its mystery, but, nonetheless, a careful study of love is possible, and, for any organization, vital. Because this data reveals that, when considering any decision or investment, the two most intelligent questions any leader should be asking themselves are:

*Will this lead to more customers loving us?*

*Will this lead to more employees loving working here?*

Of course, not every action will, but nonetheless these two questions should be the filter through which every decision is viewed. To unleash the most powerful force in business, to lead and move other people to extremely positive behaviors, you need to know how to *design love in* to the experiences you make. You're not just designing experiences; you're designing *loving* experiences. You're intentionally designing love in to the combination of touchpoints that create an experience.

This is what it means to be a DLI leader. To reject the drift into mediocrity, and instead to honor the design, the moral force, the business import, and the deeply human power of love.

# 2

# Loving versus Unloving

You can see it. We all can.

The world we're living in is not designed with us humans in mind. We sense something's wrong. The cause is hard to pin down, but it feels like chronic stress. We move through our world bombarded by an unprecedented, never-ending flood of information, by life's always-on demands, by the expectations of others, and we are brought low by this constant bombardment.

At work we are numb a lot of the time; at home we are brittle. Our own life feels like something to withstand, our days a trial to get through. We are anxious, afraid even, and to mute this fear, to turn down the volume on all that life throws at us, we medicate ourselves. We are relentlessly and mildly crushed by a world that doesn't want us, or even need us, to be us.

We cannot live like this. The sociologist Emile Durkheim in his landmark study of suicide in the late nineteenth century coined a term for our current state of mind: *anomie*. That feeling of living in a society where the norms of trust and morals have disappeared. He said that this was not a healthy state for society to be in; it was a pathological state. We humans simply cannot thrive in a trustless society. The uncertainty, the constant need to watch one's back, the permanent state of vigilance: it wears us down.

Since this is a book of hope, before we dive into how you can design love in to the experiences of those you serve and lead, I want to offer you a simple way to make sense of what's happening in the wider world. This way you can understand better what forces you're facing, and what you can do to push back against these forces. Because these forces are not irresistible. They are merely relentless—and they expand when they're accepted. When they face little resistance. But you *can* resist them if you truly live in to, and take seriously, the most powerful force in business, and life.

To begin, let's first agree on what we mean by that four-letter word. If the best leaders know how to design love in to experiences they make for others, what the heck do they mean by "love"?

## Love Is . . .

The ancient Greeks gave us eight definitions for different kinds of love, from Eros, erotic love, to Agape, universal love, but in truth there aren't eight definitions. There are eight billion, as many as there are people alive today. And yet, despite this diversity and range, as the data shows, when each one of us chooses the word *love* to define our experience, we then go on to behave in certain similarly productive ways. And the predictive power of love holds true across cultures and languages. During my time running the ADP Research Institute, our team tested various "love" survey items in twenty-eight different countries, and the data patterns remained the same across the world—Argentinians and Japanese, Saudi Arabians and South Africans all react to the word *love* in similar ways.

So, this feeling of love, though described differently by different people and peoples, must have something in common for us all. You've felt love. You've said, "I love that!" about something, or someone, or someone's actions, haven't you? We all have. Instinctively, as human beings, we all know what love feels like.

If you were to ask me today, *Marcus, from your last twenty-five years of interviews and focus groups, what do people seem to mean when they report that they "love" something, or someone, or some set of experiences?* I would offer you this definition:

> ***Love is . . . the deep and unwavering commitment to the flourishing of a human.***

So, when you say something is done "lovingly," you're saying it is done with a deep and unwavering commitment to the flourishing of a human.

When you say, "I loved that experience," you're saying it feels like the intention behind it is a deep and unwavering commitment to your flourishing.

This is a profound feeling, but you can find it in people's description of even seemingly fleeting experiences. When you say, "I love that movie!" your use of the word *love* isn't hyperbole for something you found "entertaining." You choose the word *love* because something about the movie moved you in such a human way that you felt lifted up, more connected to others, more you, more understood, even wiser, after you'd seen it. Whether it was the story, the main character, or perhaps the dynamics of one particular scene, you loved it because it touched you. In some indescribable but recognizable way, the movie helped you flourish. Obviously each of us loves different movies or books, or songs, but all of us latch on to the word *love* when the content somehow makes us feel bigger.

Or it might apply to more personal and meaningful experiences. When you say you love doing a certain activity, you commit to this word because, again, in some indescribable but recognizable way, you know that when you're doing the activity you feel at one with yourself, at ease, in control, deeply absorbed in what you're doing. You are flourishing.

Or it might apply to the feeling that someone else creates in you. When you say you love this teacher, or this doctor, or this team, or this manager, it's because, through explicit and implicit signals, you've drawn the conclusion that they are deeply and unwaveringly committed to helping you flourish. You come away from your experience with them certain that you, the person, are the purpose. You are not just an instrument for getting something done. You are you. An actual human. And you, the actual human, your flourishing is the point of it all.

The American Management Association's slogan used to be "How to get work done through people." A worthy sentiment, perhaps, but a truly loving slogan, one shared by the world's best managers, teachers, coaches, and leaders, would invert it to "How to get people done through work." The people are the point; the work is the instrument.

When you feel this—when you've been taught by a person who sees *you* first, not your grade point average; when you've worked for a manager who looks past your performance rating to the real person beneath; when you've followed a leader who paints you personally into their picture of a better future—you feel love. And you call it as you feel it.

Love is not only predictive. It is *proactive*—which differentiates it from "care." To care for someone is to be there for them when they need you. It is reactive. If a manager is caring, they'll see you struggling with a task and offer to help. If a company is caring, they'll offer support to their local community during times of crisis: the grocery store handing out free water after a hurricane, the hotel providing shelter, the retailer donating warm clothing. If a nurse is caring, they'll respond quickly when you press the call button; the caring customer service person is the one who helps you carry your bags, or who makes it easy for you when you ask to return an item.

To be caring is to be responsive. And it is a subset of loving.

To be loving is to take the initiative. Think about any person in your life who created for you an experience you'd call loving. They took action, didn't they? The family member you loved not only drove you to the ice rink at 5 a.m. every morning; they were also the one who encouraged you to try out for the hockey team in the first place. The teacher you loved not only gave you advice on how to finish the poem-writing assignment; they were the one who took your poem and, unbeknownst to you, entered it into the statewide literature contest. The manager you loved not only welcomed you onto the team; they were the one who, once they'd seen how you think and act, switched the roles around on the team so that you could play to your natural strengths more of the time.

The manager you loved might also have been the one who fired you. They were the one who took the initiative to sit you down and deliver the hard-to-hear news that "this role isn't right for you. I'm going to move you out of it because I want you to be successful and you won't be if I leave you in it." Possibly, at the time, you pushed back. You felt threatened, scared for what this might mean for you, your pride was hurt, your future uncertain. But now, in retrospect, you see the path you've since taken, the growth and success you've experienced, and you quietly thank them. They saw what you could not, and took the initiative. Tough love is loving nonetheless.

In fact, tough love may be the most valuable kind of love. If love is *the deep and unwavering commitment to the flourishing of a human*, there will be many times when the most loving thing to do to this human is to put them into challenging situations. Uncomfortable situations. Not random, out-of-their-comfort-zone situations: that isn't loving at all. But situations where their particular strengths can be called upon to flex and stretch in new ways? Yes, that is loving. The tension between the current state of a person's strengths, and what those strengths can grow to become, this is how true flourishing happens.

Though, to be clear, being loving doesn't necessarily mean being the deliverer of critical feedback. Sometimes love can be felt in an experience where the person took the initiative to *not* share something—because they knew that sharing this "feedback" would stunt your flourishing.

One of the very few teachers I loved learning from was Michael Hetherington. Among his many duties, he was charged with preparing me for my Latin entrance exam for Cambridge. I was taking the Oxbridge exam, as it's called, a year early and so each evening, outside of regular classroom hours, for the six months prior to the exam, I would go into his office by myself and attempt various pieces of Latin translation, which Mr. Hetherington would then mark up.

For those six months he would share very little about my progress. I would turn my translations in. He would read and correct. We would talk about what worked in my translations and what didn't. He'd give me another piece to translate . . . and off we'd go again. Roman rinse-and-repeat.

Months later, after I'd finally received the acceptance letter, an assembly was held, as was the custom in my school, to announce which graduates were moving on to which universities. When it was my turn, and Mr. Hetherington was called up on stage to share his thoughts, he took a small notebook from his jacket and began to read:

> "September 5th, 9:06 p.m.," he said in his nasally voice. "Marcus rushes his translations. He guesses rather than thinks it through.
>
> October 16th, 9:30 p.m. We struggled for an hour with a simple piece by Catullus. Marcus showing few signs of progress. Gives up too quickly.
>
> November 1st, 9:15 p.m. He has no chance at Cambridge at this rate. Still giving up."

I can remember standing on that stage and thinking, *I didn't know he kept a notebook. Didn't know he was writing in it such damning commentary.*

I was confused and embarrassed, trying to laugh along with the rest of the students, as Mr. Hetherington used his notes as the jumping-off point for a story of me persevering in the face of my struggles. Which was sweet of him. But the thing was, I had no idea I was struggling. I thought I was doing just fine. Which is why I kept at it. I thought back to those dark English winter nights, and tried to imagine what his commentary would have done to my spirits. I don't do well in the face of negativity; I thrive best when encouraged and challenged. I knew I would've shut down if he'd have shared it with me back then.

He knew it too. Which is why he didn't.

I have never loved a teacher more than in my realization of his restraint. For him, my flourishing was the point; his opinions could wait.

Lovingly, then, doesn't mean gently or caringly or warmly. A loving experience isn't necessarily one that makes you laugh, or feels easy, or entertains you. Nor is it always a challenging experience, even though love can sometimes be tough.

Instead, a loving experience is always and only one where, in ways large and small, you open up. A loving action is one that's undertaken to help you bloom, to expand your agency, your capability, your sense of yourself. A loving mindset is one that sees you—that sees each human—as an utterly unique combination of possibilities, and the blossoming of these possibilities as the moral starting point for everything.

Each human senses and values their own possibilities, and so, no matter our nationality, gender, race, or age, each of us is drawn to loving experiences. We know we have something inside us, and we hold out hope that the world will give us chances to express what's inside. We don't want it stuck in there. We don't want it unexpressed. We don't want to reach old age and look back and wonder why we wound up living some second-rate version of someone else's life. We want to live a first-rate version of our own. We want what's inside us to come out. And so, whenever we bump into an experience that allows us to open up, even a little, we lean in to it. And call it "loving." From the most trivial—"I love these shoes because when I wear them, I feel amazing!"—to the most meaningful—"I love this leader because they helped me believe in the best of myself!"—we recognize these loving experiences.

We use "love" not in reference to the size of the impact of the experience, but to its intimacy, with us and the expression of what's inside us. We yearn for all loving experiences, no matter their size. And when we find them, we thrive.

In your own life, you can test this out for yourself. When you hear yourself saying "Yes, loved that!" pause for a moment to look at why you picked the word "love."

When you find yourself sending a red heart emoji—not a thumbs-up, not a white or blue heart, a red one—stop and ask yourself why it felt natural to you to go with that particular expression of your feelings.

What I think you will find is that your "loved that's!" and your red hearts are neither careless nor random. They are sparked by a specific ingredient in the experience: in ways small or large, fleeting or momentous, the experience made you feel bigger. You opened up. You felt love.

Now more than ever, we need to pay attention to these loving experiences, to honor them, to understand them, to learn how to make them for ourselves and for others. Because we are—in different ways and at varying speeds—slouching toward an increasingly unloving world.

## The Experience Continuum

As we live and work in this darkening world, all of our experiences can be thought of as falling somewhere along a moral continuum (figure 2-1).

On the far left, you can find experiences in which a person or a group of people is being exploited for someone else's gain. You can imagine which sorts of experiences live at this immoral extreme. And none of us want any part of them.

What we want are experiences that live at the far-right end of the continuum. We want loving experiences. Each of us feels we have so much to give, so much to contribute and express, and we are drawn toward any experience that feels like it might help us.

**FIGURE 2-1**

**The LoveThat Experience Continuum**

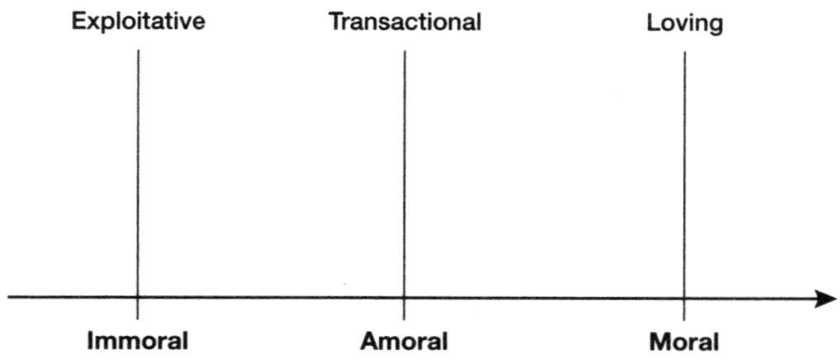


LoveThat is the trademark of the applied work of the Buckingham Institute, translating its research on human experience into practice.

*Source:* The Buckingham Institute.

From that cashier remembering our name and our favorite apple, to that teacher quietly entering our poem into a statewide contest, to that manager going to bat for us in our promotion application, we yearn for flourishing experiences.

Of course, we are realistic. We know the world won't always manufacture perfect outcomes for us: we might not find the right apples, or win the poem contest, or get the promotion. Nonetheless we are drawn to any experience focused on our flourishing.

But where do we actually live? Where do the majority of our experiences locate themselves on this continuum?

We live mostly in the middle, don't we? It started early. In school. From the age of about nine onward your unique quirks were submerged beneath the quest for uniform learning standards. Your classes were designed to produce good grades rather than a psychologically healthy human taught by teachers you loved. By the time you were thirteen, most of your conversations with your teachers and parents were spent not on your flourishing, but on your grade point average.

Upon graduating into the workplace, your flourishing continued to be largely irrelevant. As an employee you are referred to not as a whole human—with unique hopes, and strengths, and dreams. You are, instead, an FTE. A full-time equivalent. For your entire life cycle at a company, from hire, to performance and promotion, to leave or retirement, you are referred to merely as your cost to the business. They count your head: hence headcount.

As a customer, you are viewed in a similar way. You are understood to be a resource to be maximized, rather than a person to be seen and understood. At the grocery store you are your "average basket size." On the plane you are less a passenger than an asset—whose necessarily undivided attention during a flight can be turned into credit card applications or personalized advertising data. Your long-term loyalty to this particular company or brand may feel to you like a genuine emotional connection—your identity is intertwined with the brand—but to them you are simply your "lifetime customer value."

In so many parts of your life your experiences reinforce, through language, ritual, and process, that you are not a human whose flourishing is the fundamental moral starting point. You are instead an element inside a financial transaction. And so your world functions, for the most part, as an amoral ecosystem where your humanity is reduced to a countable resource, and where the fixation is not "How can we help you flourish?" but instead "How much value can we extract?"

The chief problem with your world isn't that it's immoral; at least I hope it isn't: you are not being systematically exploited. The problem with your world—with all our worlds—is that it's *amoral.* It has lost sight of you and your moral worth. Your world isn't designed for your flourishing; it's designed to extract value from transactions—between the school and its customer, the college; between the worker and the workplace; between the customer and the company. Your role is simply to try to find your place within this amoral, extractive, transactional ecosystem—and the best you can hope for is that this place doesn't alienate you from yourself too completely or too painfully.

The challenge for you, and for so many of us, is that finding a healthy place in this amoral ecosystem is hard. The best word to describe our current mental state might be *demoralized*. We are living in an amoral world, where the basic moral worth of each human—student, patient, customer, or employee—has been designed out. And for us humans it's demoralizing to live in a de-moraled world.

So, what can you do? Well, in the rest of the book, we'll dive into how you can remake your own world. But here's a technique you can use for spotting and pushing back against the wider world's bland amorality. From now on, and for the rest of your life, discipline yourself to look at the world through a DLI lens. This lens has but one function: to sort every experience into either loving or unloving.

> Loving experiences make you feel bigger.
>
> Unloving experiences make you feel smaller.
>
> Loving experiences make you feel safe enough to open up.
>
> Unloving experiences make you feel on edge, protective, like a porcupine with their quills out.
>
> While unloving experiences might help you function, loving experiences help you flourish.
>
> Loving experiences are intelligent, moral, and good for business.
>
> Unloving experiences are prosaic, amoral, and, over time, bad for business.

This lens will free you from confused feelings of *I can't quite put my finger on it, but that felt off to me!* Instead, you'll know *Ah yes, it felt off because it was unloving.*

This lens will give you more control over your world. Rather than walking into an experience that confuses, disappoints, or even hurts you, you'll be able to call it by its real name: unloving. And as Confucius long ago reminded us, calling things by their real name is the beginning of wisdom. And thus, of wise action. The naming of commonplace things as unloving will help you predict what you're in for, prepare yourself for it, and crucially, pinpoint what can be done to mitigate it.

And on the flip side, this lens will help you see what's possible in the world. It will show you what loving experiences you deserve, and what you can do to demand or design these experiences for yourself. It will show you what you can take a stand for. What you can raise your voice for. What you can strive for.

To sharpen your view through this lens, let's take a look at some of the most frequently occurring—and depleting—examples of unloving experiences. And the strategies a DLI leader can use to mitigate them.

## Handoffs Are Unloving

Think about the last time you went to your doctor.

You made your appointment with the scheduler a couple of weeks ago, and now you're sitting here in the waiting room, a little anxious. You're concerned about your health, yes, and also about whether you're going to succeed in explaining to the doctor what your exact symptoms are so that you can get exactly the right advice and prescription. The receptionist calls your name; she then hands you off to the scheduler, who then calls for the nurse practitioner, who walks you down to a particular examination room, and then leaves. Only to be replaced by a different nurse who takes your vitals and asks you a few questions, and then finally the actual doctor enters the room and administers to your health. The doctor isn't the last person you see. After they've gone you're handed off to the billing person who asks for your insurance and payment information, and then tosses you back to the scheduler who asks you if and when you want another appointment. And then you get to leave.

Six handoffs in one doctor's visit.

These handoffs work for the doctor. They are efficient and cost-effective: these days many doctors have to see one patient every seven minutes in order to make enough money to pay off their debts. But they don't work for you. You are looking for an experience that can reassure you that you, the whole person, are being seen, and heard, and helped. You are not your symptom. You are not "the gallbladder in exam room 2." You are you, with a life, a lifestyle, a personality, a history, and a future. You want an experience, particularly one focused on your health, that takes all of this into account.

And each handoff increases the stressful feeling that it doesn't. Each handoff forces you to question whether this new person understands your whole story. Each handoff puts the burden back on you to explain yourself again and again. Trying to remember all the important details, even though, if you're being honest, you don't know which details are important and which aren't. Each handoff feels to you like pressing the C button on a calculator—your whole-person "numbers" all disappear and you find yourself starting your narrative from scratch, with the scheduler, the nurse practitioner, the other nurse, the doctor, C, C, C, C, all of your carefully constructed set of details and understandings erased, reduced to zero, again, and again, and again.

Wherever we bump into them, handoffs make experiences unloving. When you went out for dinner last night, how did it feel when you got handed off from the host stand to the busser, to the waiter, to the food delivery folks, and then back to the waiter? Didn't it feeling jarring that, though your waiter took your actual order, when you and your partner switched places because the AC was blowing on them too hard, the food runner, unaware of which actual human ordered which meal, placed your food in front of your partner, and vice versa? And then, when you needed a refill of your water glass or your wine, didn't it feel odd that, when you asked that nice person to help you, they smiled and said, "I'm sorry, I'm the busser. Let me pass that along to your server"?

Sure, these handoffs weren't soul-destroying, but each, in its own small way, was unloving. Each communicated to you that you were not an actual human; you were merely "Table 4." An actual human would obviously be stressed to discover that no one person was taking care of them, and that, instead, their needs were being relayed like a game of telephone across seven or eight different people. But, no, you're just Table 4—and of course, the most efficient way to transact with Table 4 is to hand the table off to one person after another.

Try to buy a car, or go to hospital, or call your airline, and you'll experience this same unloving handoff from the salesperson to the sales manager, to the finance manager, to the technician.

Each human wants a single point of contact, someone who can get to know the details of their life and their needs, and figure out a tailored solution. And yet every experience seems to have been designed for multiple points of contact. I've even heard it suggested that these handoffs are part of a deliberate strategy, now commonly known as "sludge," designed to so frustrate the person that in the end they give up their quest—for a refund, a change in their reservation, a company resource, or even their access to a government program. Sludging—the passing of the employee or customer from one robo-agent, to one representative, to another department, to a supervisor, and back again, with each new contact requiring the person's retelling of their story—seems practical. It may even generate cost savings, at least in the short term. But, to call it by its real name, it is unloving. And because love is the most powerful predictor of productive human behaviors, it is bad business.

By revealing handoffs as unloving, and thus bad business, we create the need for action: putting the moral issues aside, no effective leader should ever let stand something so destructive to business value. In this case, you don't have to get rid of all handoffs; this isn't sensible or practical. It does mean, though, that you'll want to figure out the best ways to mitigate the unloving nature of handoffs so they don't continue to destroy so much value.

Back in 1996 Dr. Robert Wachter and Dr. Lee Goldman devised one such mitigation strategy. Confronting the sorry state of patient outcomes in many US hospitals, they realized that it might be helpful to create a role dedicated to serving the holistic needs of each hospitalized patient. In between the patient and the serial list of specialist physicians, they would insert a person who could explain the whole patient to the physicians, and the physicians to the patient. This person would themselves be a physician, but their job would be the story link from one physician handoff to the next. The patient would no longer have to struggle to play this role themselves. Instead, the professional explainer would hold the patient's story and relay it in the right way, to the right people.

This person came to be called the hospitalist. And it was so successful in dramatically improving patient outcomes that it spawned its own movement—the hospitalist movement—and is now a cornerstone of modern hospital medicine.

When we call out an experience as unloving, this doesn't mean we have to stop doing it. It does mean that it's unacceptable and unintelligent to leave it as is. That we need to apply all our creativity to figure how to turn unloving to loving. Innovations such as Dr. Wachter and Dr. Goldman's show us how doable and how powerful such innovations can be.

## Shape-Shifting Is Unloving

In late 2023 Delta Airlines announced that they would be changing their frequent flier program. From now on, they said, you will earn frequent flier points based less on how many miles you flew on Delta, and more on how many dollars you spent on the Delta credit card.

This decision was made after an exhaustive analysis by the Boston Consulting Group on how to maximize the value of each passenger's behavior, and therefore which behaviors to incentivize. The conclusion: in the calculus of how to maximize you in your transactions with Delta, you are more valuable to them as a spender than as a passenger. And so the frequent flier program became a frequent spender program.

There is nothing immoral about Delta doing this to its program. They are making a rational and amoral decision to extract as much value as possible from an abundant resource in their business ecosystem: their passengers.

Nonetheless this just feels off, doesn't it? Delta can do whatever it wants to its loyalty programs, but, really, they're now going to reward spending over flying?

Look through the DLI lens and you see that what's wrong with this decision is that it's unloving. A loving experience is one where you know where you stand. You know what to expect from the person or the situation, or, in this case, the company. Clarity is a deeply loving thing to give someone. You can't flourish if you can't trust whom you're relying on, and for what. When a company, or a person, shape-shifts who they are for you, your instinctive human reaction is to close ranks, withdraw, and, like an armadillo rolling up inside its armored shell, do what's necessary to protect yourself.

Delta shape-shifted who they were for people.

And it wasn't a small shift; it wasn't a tweak to a loyalty program. It was a seismic shift. People entered into a relationship with Delta as passengers. They turned to Delta to provide excellent passenger-related experiences, such as, among other things, flying. By changing their loyalty program from flying to spending, they were fundamentally changing who they were for people. They were saying, unintentionally perhaps, *We are not an airline. We are a bank. And so from now on, you are not passengers. You are . . . well, we aren't entirely sure what you are. But can you please sign up for and use our credit card.*

United Airlines has done similar shape-shifting, and it feels similarly unloving. They have decided that one excellent way to maximize you in your transaction with them is to sell your eyeballs to other companies. Yes, you are still a passenger, but to United the most valuable aspect of you being a passenger is that you're forced to stare at the seatback in front of you. Your coerced attention is an asset—over which you have little control. And when you combine this with something else you can't control, namely the personal data that, by law, you are required to share with them, then voilà, United has a product to sell: your personal data to other companies who can then show you personalized ads in that seatback you're staring at. Or, in the words of the person who runs United's frequent flier program: "We've built a first-of-its-kind, real-time, adtech-enabled traveler media network where brands have already started connecting to premium audiences at an unmatched scale."

As with Delta's plan, there is nothing necessarily exploitative about United's new "adtech-enabled traveler media network" but it is amoral. It does fundamentally shift who United is for its passengers. It is unloving. And so it will, over time, degrade United's relationship with its passengers.

Just as Delta's did. Which is why so many passengers pushed back on Delta. And why, despite spending hundreds of millions of dollars in the design and launch of their new frequent spender program, Delta was forced to reverse course almost immediately.

If you want more loving experiences in your life, you can do the same—with United, or Delta, or any company that shape-shifts who they are for you. You can call it out as unloving, and then vote with your feet or your wallet. If you don't mind being treated unlovingly, if you are just fine with being seen mostly as an element in a transactional equation, you can keep doing business with unloving companies. But if, as consumers of experiences, we want to exert our power in the world, and dispel our feelings of anomie, it's up to us to label things as they really are: unloving or loving.

So when the CEO of Delta apologizes with "We went too far. Your response made clear that the changes did not fully reflect the loyalty you have demonstrated to Delta," we can all raise our voices and say simply: *Delta, what you did was unloving. It was bad for us humans. And bad business. Do better.*

## Large Spans of Control Are Unloving

Have you ever wondered why we see such high burnout rates in nurses? We are often told that the secret to living a deeply fulfilling life is to find your purpose, your "why." You would think that nurses have this covered. They are so close every minute of every day to the purpose of what they do. Yes, the work is challenging, and the hours long, but at least they feel a clear sense of mission every day, in the eyes of each patient and family member.

Why then are nurses, of all the groups of workers I have ever studied, the least engaged at work?

During the pandemic, and since, as we continue to struggle nationally and globally with chronic nurse shortages, I've heard many different explanations: low wages, inherently stressful situations, obnoxious doctors, labyrinthine data-record systems. Each must play a part. But the main cause of nurse burnout isn't on this list, and rarely, if ever gets a mention: large spans of control.

Want to know the average span of control in modern American hospitals, nurse supervisor to nurse? It's one-to-forty. One nurse supervisor to forty nurses.

Nurses, as all humans do, require attention to flourish. They want to be in a team environment where their team leader can get to know them—their name, their life situation, their strengths and weaknesses, their emotional state, their rhythms and rituals, how they learn, how they deal with change. How can the poor nurse supervisor pay attention closely enough to learn all of this when they have forty humans on their "team"?

They can't. And so they don't. Each nurse comes into work every day knowing that they are unseen, unheard, unfelt. If they are struggling with processing a particularly stressful situation from yesterday, they will have no one to share this with today. If they are worried about their relationship with a certain physician, the nurse supervisor doesn't have the time to hear about it. If there's a conflict between them and another team member, it festers.

The other day I was interviewing a chief human resources officer for a large health-care system in the northeast. "Our average span of control in some places is one to sixty," she said. "I was talking to a nurse who'd been with us for twenty-three years and she told me that most of the people at work didn't even know her name!"

Can you imagine going to work in such an isolating environment? Perhaps you don't have to imagine it. Perhaps you work in a manufacturing plant or a call center where the spans of control are just as large as for nurses. It's draining, isn't it? You're among people, but basically you're alone. You might be able to stick it out for a while, but over time it becomes deeply demoralizing. And one day you can't get out of bed and go to work anymore.

These sorts of spans of control are not immoral, nor even exploitative. But they are unloving. Their irreparable fail point is their inability to allow each whole human to receive the attention all humans need. They might work on a balance sheet. They do not work for humans. And they never will.

Again, you may still choose to work for such a place, or through force of your circumstances, you may have no choice. But wherever we see these large spans of control we should call them by their name: they are unloving. And so, in the end, they are bad business.

As labor markets get tighter and tighter, the power will shift toward the worker, toward you and me. It will be up to us to pressure workplaces to implement practices that create loving experiences for us, experiences whose purpose is to help us flourish. Each organization can address this differently, but few will do it at all unless we raise our collective voice and label current practices accurately: loving or unloving. Good business or bad business. Let's all learn to call organizations' practices by their real name. And then each of us can decide if we want to work for a place that takes seriously the most powerful force in business—or one that doesn't.

And if you happen to be a leader in an organization with such large spans of control, the burden lies with you to name it as unloving—and therefore as unintelligent and unprofitable—and then to design experiences to mitigate it.

One such organization can be found in that health-care system in the Northeast. Upon discovering how stressed out and isolated their nurses were, and knowing that they couldn't afford to create an entirely new layer of management to give each nurse attention, they instead created a cluster of informal twelve-person teams, with one carefully chosen person on each team designated as the go-to for everyone else on the team. This person wasn't an official supervisor. They were simply a person who loved connecting with others, and who could check in with each person at the start of the shift, listen to what was on each person's heart and mind, and, when necessary, convey anything urgent up to the nurse supervisor.

This go-to role didn't add cost. It did add value. It gave the nurses the attention they needed—and it gave the hospital a new role to offer to those particular people who loved connecting with others.

Neither of which would have happened, of course, if the leaders hadn't looked through the DLI lens, seen the one-to-sixty ratio as unloving, and got creative about how to fix it.

## Outsourcing Is Unloving

I went to a Coldplay concert recently and I'm afraid I wouldn't tell you to do the same. Not that I didn't love the music: I've been a fan of Coldplay since their first album *Parachutes* came out in 2000, and some of the songs since then are way up there on my forever playlist. And yes, wow, they can sure put on a show. Chris Martin leaps around the stage like a buzzing, blue-arsed fly (as my mom would say) and what with the illuminating bracelets, the Glastonbury-like flag waving, and the fireworks, it's a glorious two-hour sing-along assault on the senses.

But no, I wouldn't tell you to go yourself.

You see, like every experience, this one had a sequence to it. A sequence that I—and every other human at this concert—was moving through. It began with me going online and trying to find the right seats, the right price, and the right day. Then I had to transfer the tickets from the seller to my phone, and buy the parking pass on offer. Then we drove down to the stadium, early to avoid the traffic, passed through security, found our seats, grabbed something to eat and drink—all "fair trade" products because of Chris's stance on such things—and settled in for the show.

The "during" part of the experience was the show itself—which was magic. And during which Chris made sure to thank us all for carving time out of our busy lives to come see them play, and which featured a rather touching couple of songs where he asked us all to turn off our phones and cameras and simply experience the experience with our eyes and ears and swaying bodies. A clichéd request, you might say, but when fifty thousand people stop clicking and flashing, and start paying attention, you really feel it. Perhaps because these days you feel it so rarely.

Then it was over.

The "after" of the experience was the getting-out-of-the-parking-lot part. This part took longer than the entire concert. All of the carefully choreographed, multisensory touchpoints of the concert experience disappeared as we bumped our cars and gritted our teeth and stressed out about picking the right serpentine line snaking around the stadium. It couldn't have been a more jarring experience from the warmhearted, communal love-in of the concert. What was once thousands of bracelets glowing as one was now every person for themselves, as we bumper-car'd our way back onto the freeway, and fought our way home.

Coldplay had nothing to do with the parking. Coldplay hadn't thought about the parking. Because Coldplay had outsourced the parking. They'd handed it off to someone else. And this someone had then ruined the experience for the rest of us.

And who can blame Coldplay for outsourcing the parking? Chris Martin doesn't know parking! Of course they outsourced it! Terrible parking ingress and egress is just what we expect when we go to a concert, and, as when Ticketmaster charges us far above the face value of the tickets, we surely don't blame the artist for the frustrating parking experience. We just accept it.

And yet they had thought quite carefully about other aspects of the experience. They'd brought flags, and bracelets, and fireworks. They'd asked us to turn off our phones. They'd even made sure that all the merchandise on sale was fair trade. All so that we could have a carefully curated experience during the concert.

But when it came to another part of the experience—which all us humans would have to go through—they'd drawn a line in their mind, stopped designing and curating, and instead handed it off to someone else.

You might say, well, come on, if the concert is fantastic who cares how hard it was to leave? We're all just going to put up with it.

But in this interconnected age, the lines demarking who is responsible for what are becoming increasingly fuzzy, and the ability to voice our displeasure about an experience is becoming increasingly easy. In the summer of 2025 during Post Malone and Jelly Roll's concert series, they booked a couple of nights at Thunder Ridge, an outdoor venue in the Ozarks. It's a beautiful setting looking out over Table Rock Lake, with seating for close to twenty thousand fans. Unfortunately, more than a third of them never made it to the concert. The access roads hadn't been properly prepared for that weight of traffic, nor had they organized enough parking spots, and this oversight, plus a couple of inevitable car accidents on the roads, led to thousands of people stranded in their cars. The final five miles took, on average, five hours. These thousands of disappointed concert-non-goers then took to social media to share their anger with tens of millions of others.

Technically this wasn't Post or Jelly's "fault"—any more than it's your employer's fault that the payroll company they outsourced your paycheck to messed up your tax withholding, or your insurer's fault that your hospital ordered a test that wasn't covered by your plan. But, in our own mind, these distinctions, these lines drawn between certain parts of our experience, are becoming blurred. We might not be sure whom to blame, but when large chunks of our experience have been outsourced, we aren't reluctant to take matters into our own hands and tell millions of our friends and followers how awful the experience was.

So, while we can feel bad for Post and Jelly, and Chris and Coldplay, that they're being held accountable for experiences beyond their control, the most relevant takeaway for them—and for you—is that taking *all* aspects of an experience seriously is a loving thing to do. It shows that you are aware that a whole human is having this experience, and they will experience the experience as a whole human moving through each part of it. If Chris had thought about the experience in this way—through the lens of one human moving through different parts of an experience—he might have done things differently with the parking. Losing sight of the whole human, and instead dissecting the experience into separate parts of a process—seat selection, to ticket purchase, to ticket redemption, to merchandise sales, to the actual concert, to the parking and exiting—each outsourced to a separate entity, is an unloving thing to do. It puts all the pressure on each human to knit these experiences together into a coherent whole—which is hard to do when the entities responsible for each part apparently don't talk to one another.

It's intriguing that some artists—noncoincidentally, those with the most passionate fans—have decided that this sort of outsourcing is unacceptable. Taylor Swift, upset by the pricing practices of Ticketmaster, created her own fan-facing program, TaylorSwiftTix, to distribute, swap, and share tickets among her fans without the malign presence of scalping bots and their massive markups. Pearl Jam were the pioneers in this—boycotting Ticketmaster back in the mid-nineties—and, more recently, The Cure, AC/DC, and Metallica have all tried to protect their fans from negative ticket-buying experiences by bringing ticket sales in-house.

To be clear, I'm not suggesting we should stop all outsourcing, and bring everything in-house—Coldplay should probably not get into the parking business. But, if they are going to outsource it, then they should look through the DLI lens, name it unloving, and then do everything they can to mitigate its inherent unloving-ness.

How? Well, as is always the case with outsourcing, the best double-barreled mitigation strategy is *selection and education*. Coldplay could have carefully selected the parking vendor, worked with them to create as detailed a plan for exiting us as they had done for entertaining us or for picking the fair trade products, and then required the vendor to educate all their workers on what the "Coldplay experience" was supposed to feel like. In its entirety. From start to finish.

This is what all great experience-design companies do whenever their business strategy requires them to outsource. Chick-fil-A is the most profitable quick-service restaurant in the world not just because of their chicken sandwiches, but because they have created a sequence of experiences that surround the sandwich: the team members seem happier, the leaders are ever-present, the chorus of "It's my pleasure's" greets every customer. They have won the American Customer Satisfaction Index award for most-beloved quick-service restaurant company for eleven straight years.

And yet none of these team members or leaders actually works for Chick-fil-A. Each restaurant is independently owned. They've outsourced every single brick and mortar and human manifestation of their experience.

*Selection and education* explain how they still manage to deliver at scale such extreme positive experiences. They make it so extraordinarily difficult to become a restaurant operator that today it is, statistically speaking, harder to become one than it is to get into Harvard. And then, for those precious few who do get selected, they dedicate thousands of hours per year per leader to their education in all things hospitality and experience-design.

So, yes, while outsourcing is unloving, the labeling of it as such doesn't restrict you. Instead, it frees you to think creatively about what else you can and should do to make loving experiences. The labeling of outsourcing as unloving, and therefore as value-depleting, spurs you to figure out new and practical ways to create love in the hearts of those you serve.

In contrast, by averting our eyes from what is unloving we allow ourselves to become accepting of—even complicit in—the value and values-depletion of our current world. These days we just accept that the makers of our experiences started with the process, not the human. We accept that they broke down the elements of the process into separate bits, handed off each bit to different departments, and then left the burden on each human to figure out how to turn all these bits into an actual experience.

At work, human resources departments serve as a dispiriting example. It used to be that each employee would have an HR generalist inside their company. This generalist would be available to the employee no matter what question or issue they might have, would come to know the employee personally, and, once they'd listened to the employee's needs—a paycheck issue perhaps, or a family leave request, or an employee relations problem—they'd hand the employee off to the specialist HR department that could meet their need.

Today the HR generalist is no more. What's replaced them is a set of parallel processes, each designed as though ignorant of the existence of the others.

If you have a paycheck issue, you are given an 800 number to call, and a voice on the other end who most likely doesn't even work for your company. Why? Because your company has outsourced all pay-related matters. Why? Because it was cost-effective.

If you have an employee-leave issue—perhaps because you are looking for maternity leave, or to take time to care for your mom—you get a different number to call. This voice doesn't know you, or your family situation, or anything about your manager, your work, your team, because this voice works for the insurance agency your company outsourced all their benefits administration to. Why? Because it was more efficient.

Over the last thirty years the HR function has literally disintegrated itself. The CEO wanted all the people stuff to be handled cost-effectively and efficiently, the HR technology companies were eager to oblige, and so now your actual experience as an employee is itself disintegrated.

It's all so very demoralizing. And so now is the right time for all of us to label it properly: outsourcing is unloving. We can then either ask our workplace to do better, and mitigate the outsourcing by intentionally designing experiences with the whole human in mind—or we can go find other workplaces that are more serious about designing love in.

What we do at our peril is passively accept it.

## AI Is . . .

The AI train is barreling down the tracks, scaring us, exciting us, and making a heck of a din. It can write poems, detect climate-changing weather patterns, and quasi-translate whale song. Pew has predicted that nearly one in five US workers is in a job highly likely to be transformed by AI. It is the ultimate game-changer.

And yes, we are all rightly worried about certain aspects of AI. How will it change our jobs? And which jobs? Whose data is it using to train itself on? How might it be used to create fake facts, fake pictures, fake people, and how will any of us be able to tell fact from fiction? Will it ever develop consciousness—so-called artificial general intelligence—and how will we control it then? What are the ethics of keeping a conscious entity in bondage? If we set it free, how do we stop it from taking over the world? Or how do we stop bad actors from taking it over, faking us out, and then they take over the world?

For your purposes, a leader striving for mastery in DLI, this is one question to grapple with: Is AI loving or unloving, and if the latter, can it ever be trained to be loving?

Asking if AI can be loving is not the same question as asking if you can love AI. Yes, you can love AI—in the same way that you can love any inanimate thing that helps you express something inside you. You can love AI because it helps you organize your thoughts, or discover important facts and the connections between these facts, or saves you time, or presents your thoughts in compelling words, images, slides, or graphs.

In contrast, asking if AI itself is loving means considering this: Can AI, through either its design or its execution, actually bring more love into our experiences? If we train customer service chatbots on certain datasets, can they deliver loving experiences? Can we teach AI doc-bots to heal us lovingly? Can AI educators learn to teach us lovingly? When it comes to our interactions with this thing called AI, can it actually bring more love into the interaction?

Not "Can we love it?" but can we feel that it loves us? Can it be the creator, the initiator, the source of loving experiences?

Given what you now know about the power of love to drive productive human behaviors, these are not esoteric questions. If a company inserts AI into more and more of its functions and processes, will it get more of these productive behaviors from customers and employees or less?

As a guide for you, a leader in these radically changing times, you might consider these two factors as you contemplate how, where, and if AI can bring more love in.

## Optimize AI for love

One big debate in AI is whether it should be "aligned" or "unaligned." That is, do we let it run free and see where it leads itself? This is "unaligned." Or do we try to curtail its negative impulses (such as choosing to blackmail employees using the content of their emails once it learned that these employees were going to shut it down—a very scary, and very real example) by "aligning" it to a certain humanistic value system?

This framing makes for an interesting debate, but it's actually a red herring. AI will never be unaligned. It will always be aligned to someone, or some group's value system, because AI is, at bottom, a machine for optimizing for certain outcomes. It can be trained to optimize for any number of outcomes, from efficiency, to accuracy, to politeness, to security, to speed—the list is unending. And so, the real question is: If AI can be optimized for anything, which group, and which values, determine what precisely it should be optimized for?

My recommendation is that, among other priorities, it should always be optimized for love. If we can identify which feelings comprise the overall feeling of love, let's then train our AI tools to optimize for creating those feelings. Yes, we know that this email from our bank was written by AI, but, optimized for love, this AI email might use phrases, framings, and tone to conjure in our hearts the beginnings of loving feelings. Likewise, we know that this chatbot is powered by AI, but if it has been trained to interact with us lovingly, do we care that it isn't a real human—particularly if it is up front with us that it's a bot, and that it is simply and non-passive-aggressively trying to do its best for us?

It will be interesting to see how all of us respond to AI tools optimized for love, but surely, they can't be worse at creating loving experiences than grumpy, poorly trained customer service agents who have been incentivized to "sludge" us.

In the next chapter we'll dive into the five feelings at the heart of love. It could well be that an AI trained to shape each of these feelings winds up doing precisely that—even while we know that the AI has no idea what true human flourishing feels like.

## A new ROI: Return on intent

At a recent *Wall Street Journal* gathering a chief marketing officer was asked about her use of AI:

> I love it. I used it to write my performance reviews last week. I mean, brilliant, right? Last week I had to write twenty-six reviews by 9 p.m. otherwise our AI-powered review tool would

> shut me out. So, I put the basic meat of my thoughts into it, and then it revised them, formatted them, made me sound smart, made my feedback sound incredible. So long as you're using it as a personal productivity tool, I think it's great. What do I need more of? I need more time. How am I going to get through twenty-six reviews? AI!

Twenty-six performance reviews! Putting aside whether completing such reviews is a good use of time for an expensive resource such as a CMO, you can see why she loves AI. It saved her from a massive time suck. It helped her get out from under an HR administrative burden so she could focus her brain on more value-adding matters. Her experience is all of our experience with AI—we love it because it gives us our time back, and makes us look smart in the process.

But take a moment to consider the twenty-six people who received her AI-generated reviews. What did they feel? Do you think they noticed that the words and phrasings weren't her own? If they did, do you think they cared? Would you have cared?

The term of art for a body of text generated by AI—whether in a performance review, an English paper, a company announcement, or a customer email—is "slop." Academic institutions are currently in an arms race with AI large language models to devise software that can detect AI slop with 100 percent accuracy, and they are losing. But for you, a leader trying to create extreme positive outcomes, the issue is less *Can I detect slop accurately?* and more *How does it make people feel when they suspect slop?*

In our working definition of love—*the deep and unwavering commitment to the flourishing of a human*—the word *commitment* implies a connection, and an authentic intention behind that connection. If we suspect that your words directed toward us are not your own, if we suspect they're slop, do we also start to suspect your intentions toward us? And if we don't go all the way to suspicion of your intentions, do we merely dismiss your intentions as unknowable, and thus break the connection between us? How does love last in a fake-first world? For the CMO leader, if the twenty-six recipients suspected that the words weren't hers, did they still find value in these words? Did they see through the fakery to the loving intentions beneath?

Obviously, I can't tell you for sure, one way or another. But for you, and for all of us, it's interesting to consider the relationship between love and intent. Without question, our feelings of love thrive in experiences where the intent of the experience is explicit rather than opaque, and flourishing-focused rather than repressive. We are far more likely to feel bigger, to open up, to risk expressing what's inside of us when we're sure that the intent of the experience is genuinely *for us*. If we suspect its intent, if we are even unsure of its intent, we will close ranks, get vigilant, and do what's necessary to protect ourselves. Genuine intent is the handmaiden of love. Artificiality, by obscuring intent, is love's antagonist.

You can feel your natural human sensitivity to intent in something as analogue as a baby blanket. If your best friend hands you a blanket she bought online, you might say, "Oh, this is so soft, and I love the color—thank you!" But if she hands you the same blanket and tells you, "My aunt made this. She crocheted it while watching her favorite old movies and thought about the baby the whole time. She's been making blankets like this for thirty years," suddenly, the blanket carries something else. It carries love's fingerprint. And that's what we humans are always scanning for. We aren't just moved by beauty, or functionality, or ease of use. We're moved by human intent. By that ineffable aura we feel when we know a human cared.

Your friend's aunt knitted genuine human love into the blanket, and you, upon receiving it, felt the love, felt the intent, and the feeling moved you. This is a feeling of connection. You are connected to her, through strands made of empathy; you could imagine her curled up in her favorite chair, needles clack-clacking, thinking about the baby. You've had these feelings, these thoughts; you've wanted to do something special for a child; you've felt your heart burst with love for all that the child could become—and now she's taken these same feelings and woven them into the blanket for your own child.

The most lovingly designed AI can simulate warmth or affirmation. It can say all the right things. But it can't carry this aura of loving intent. Can it?

What this means for you, and all DLI leaders, is that intent, and people's perception of your intent, is a valuable asset. Be deliberate about how you communicate your intent, be precise about how you mitigate the inherently artificial nature of AI, and you are much more likely to net a powerful return on your intent.

So, when you're inserting AI tools into your working world, pay attention to:

- *Transparency:* Always be transparent that something has been created by AI.
- *Mimicry:* Be careful how far to let AI go in mimicking human feelings in its language and tone.
- *Empathic overreach:* Don't allow your AI tools to overreach in expressing empathy for what an actual human is going through. We know it doesn't feel what we feel. It has nothing at stake. Has never risked. Has never felt fear, or embarrassment, or anxiety, or shame. Or love. Its faked empathy is like aspartame: sweet at first, but with that jarring metallic aftertaste.

Obviously, when it comes to AI, there's a great deal for us to learn in the coming years about the link between AI and extreme positive human behaviors. What we know now for sure is that love drives those behaviors, and that, left to its own devices, AI is not necessarily going to optimize itself to treat us lovingly. And so it will be up to leaders like you to be precise in your understanding of what loving feels like, to be protective of those feelings, and, using AI and other tools, to be proactive in creating them.

To that end, let's explore now the five feelings at the heart of love.

# 3

# The Five Feelings of Love

In middle of the seventeenth century, Sir Isaac Newton, whiling away his time in his cottage in Cambridge while the rest of England battled the plague, decided one afternoon to put a glass prism in a chink in the wall: he was interested in light, its form, its source, its ingredients. The prism-in-the-wall-chink was one of his experiments. And as you may know, what Newton saw, once the sun had peeked out from behind the watery English clouds, was a rainbow of colors arrayed on the far wall of his cottage. His prism had pulled apart white light to reveal all the spectrum of colors within. White light, he discovered, wasn't mysteriously monolithic. It was constructed from the combination of the frequencies of the other colors.

As with light, so with love. We can use psychometric research as a prism to tease love apart and reveal its ingredients. And then, as Newton did with white light, once we know in more detail what love is made of, we're in an excellent position to design it in to experiences. We'll know how to design recruiting experiences that attract the right kind of people, team experiences that get the best from these people, customer experiences that get them to fall in love with our service or product, and experiences in our own life that allow each of us to find and plug into our greatest sources of power.

I'm excited to share this with you because I think this will be one of those mental pictures that, once you've seen it, you'll never be able to unsee. You'll carry it with you for the rest of your life and use it to make sense of any experience you encounter. It will clarify what's happening—for good or for ill—and direct you toward how to make it better. Look at any experience with this mental picture in mind and you'll have a greater understanding of what's really going on, and what you as a leader can do about it.

To explore the ingredients of love, start by thinking about a person at the beginning of an experience. They might be a brand-new customer just walking into your restaurant, or a novice employee being onboarded into your company, or a twenty-year veteran calling up human resources to ask about family leave. Or perhaps this person is you, just starting a new job, or walking into work one Monday morning, or kicking off a daily huddle meeting with your team.

If you can, picture the person after their experience, and they're now walking around buoyed by love in their heart. They're the new customer who can't stop selling their friends on how marvelous your restaurant is. They're the no-longer-novice employee who's telling their family how at home they feel in their new job. They're the veteran who felt so protected during their family leave experience that they can't imagine working for anyone else. Or they're you, who's had such extremely positive experiences in your new job, or during your regular Monday morning, or at your team huddle, that your heart is full.

The question for you is: How did you get there? What happened to you to lead you to walk around with love in your heart? And what happened to those other people—the new customer, the novice employee, the veteran—to cause them to be carriers of love, spreading goodwill and good words and good actions to all they meet?

Could it just be magic, that getting someone to fall in love with your brand or your company is a magical mystery tour? That if you keep delivering on your promises, doing solid work, that good feelings build up little by little until suddenly, shazam!, they bloom into love?

Or perhaps those feelings of love were created by what's sometimes called service recovery. That you spotted how grumpy the new customer was, or the novice employee, and you then went far above and beyond to make them happy—by comping their meal perhaps, or giving them a free gift, or upgrading their seat on the plane, or, if they're an employee, by offering them a signing bonus or a surprise raise. And the chemical reaction of their grumpiness with their surprised delight sparked love.

Both of these explanations have merit. Yes, there is and always will be something magical about a person's feeling of love in their heart. And yes, who wouldn't be happy with an unexpected raise or gift?

But neither of these explanations serves us fully. Because I have to report that a careful reevaluation of the last quarter century of research into extreme positives—my version of the prism-in-the-wall-chink experiment—reveals there is something predictable about those feelings of love. Something describable, and therefore repeatable.

When I deconstructed, and reverse-engineered, how the person walking around with love in their heart actually arrived there, these two patterns emerged.

First, at the heart of a loving experience are five distinct feelings. And second, these five feelings follow a set sequence. (To review the paper detailing the research underpinning these five feelings, and their sequential nature, please visit DesignLoveIn.com.)

This means that if you can learn these five feelings, and focus on them in sequence, you will be in the best possible position to know which actions—or tools, rituals, processes, and systems—create them in yourself and others and which do not. You will know what loving experiences look like and how to make them. This is crucial for you as a leader—or, indeed, as an influencer of others—because to get people to do what you want them to do, you first have to get them to feel what you want them to feel. In this sense, these five feelings confer on you five distinct powers; in other words, you have the power to create these feelings in others, and so you have the power to move them to productive action.

Let me share them with you, and then in part two of this book we can dive into how you can create them in the lives of those you lead and serve.

To bring these five feelings to life, I've decided to use a health-care example. These five apply across all domains, but we've all been to the doctor, and we all know what's it's like to feel neutrally or negatively about our visits. And at the other extreme, we all yearn to be able to say, "I love my doctor!"

So, imagine you're the patient. I'm the doctor. What feelings do I need to create in you, sequentially, to have you emerge from your experience with love in your heart?

## 1. Control

### "What is this world, and how do I work it?"

While researching extraordinarily successful doctors during my years at the Gallup Organization, we asked patients hundreds of different questions about their experiences, ranging from the pragmatic "How long do you typically have to sit in the waiting room before seeing the doctor?" to the deeply emotional "Do you feel your doctor truly cares about you as a human being?" And in study after study, when we examined which questions were most powerful, these two emerged:

> "Did my doctor explain my condition to me in words I could understand?"
>
> "Did my doctor give me something I could do at home to alleviate my condition?"

No matter what brought them to the doctor, no matter how long they'd been seeing their doctor, the patients who answered these questions with a 5, on a 1–5 scale, were far more likely to exhibit extremely positive subsequent behaviors: they talked up the doctor to friends and family, they stayed loyal to the doctor over many years, and, most importantly, their health outcomes were consistently better.

This is the feeling of *control*. To treat you lovingly, I must start by helping you feel control. Not control over others. Control over yourself. Control over your actions and choices. As every human does, you move through life on edge. Instinctively you know that the world is massive, busy, loud, and always moving, and your fear is that the world will pick you up and spin you around, dragging you along and dumping you out in random, unfamiliar places. So, to treat you lovingly, I must respond to this on-edge feeling by giving you signs that the world you're now entering is simple and controllable.

This could mean its *purpose* is simple: I immediately help you know what my organization is trying to be, what it is trying to do for others, what it stands for, and what outcomes define its success. And the clearer I am with you about this, the more control I give you: to choose whether or not you want to enter this world, and what you should expect when you do. In our health-care example, this could mean what kind of practice I run, what sorts of patients are my main focus, or what I specialize in.

It could be *spatially* simple. For instance, I help you know where to go, which "room" you are now in, what this room is for, and which room you will enter next.

Its *guiding resources* are simple—to treat you lovingly is to know that no matter how much control you currently feel, at some point you will get lost and will need a guiding hand. So I've taken the initiative to anticipate the kinds of questions you'll need help with, and proactively shown you where, how, and who can help you answer these questions.

In your case, as my patient, you also want it to be *operationally* simple: I need to help you describe your own condition to yourself in words you can understand, and give you something you yourself can do to feel a little better. Both things ensure that you feel that the locus of control—what is happening to you right now, and what you can do to improve your health—lies within you.

Clarify your world so that you no longer feel disoriented and helpless. Give you control of your surroundings, your direction, your tools. This is the first sign of love. And whether or not you are conscious of this sign, it registers deep within you as a loving experience, and so you lean in and move closer toward love in your heart.

The inverse is also true. As we know from studies of learned helplessness, if I fail to orient you, fail to give you control over the world I am drawing you into, you will retreat—or in the case of learned helplessness, curl up into a little ball and shiver. Whether psychologically or physically, you will pull your identity back and away from my world. You will put up barriers. You will treat with suspicion my next actions, my next words, and so your subsequent behavior will be nothing like what I want from you. In the face of other offers, you won't stay loyal to me. In the face of mistakes, you won't give me the benefit of the doubt. And when questioned by friends and family, you won't advocate for me. I've lost you. On the surface you may look like any other patient of mine, but inside, because I've failed to give you the feeling of control, you are now armored against me.

As straightforward as our need for control would appear, it's astounding, and disappointing, to see how many otherwise well-intended leaders look right past it.

To give you but one example, a number of airlines have just announced—proudly—that they will be using AI to determine how much each passenger will be willing to pay for their seat. In a world blind to the power of love to drive productive human behavior, this tactic seems sensible. It lives squarely in the transactional section of the experience continuum. These airlines have decided to use AI to calculate how much can be extracted from each passenger in each transaction.

But in a world attuned to love as the most powerful force in business, these airlines would realize how value-destroying these pricing tactics are. They would recognize immediately that these AI pricing algorithms were removing all control from the passengers. That no passenger will know what their unique pricing quotient is, nor how it is calculated, nor how to change it, and that therefore, these passengers will stall in their journey toward love in their heart for the airline. The airline has ignored their need for control, has treated each passenger as merely a resource to be maximized, and so each passenger will soon come to see themselves in just the same way—as a resource to be maximized.

And then these airlines will scratch their heads and wonder: *In the hypercompetitive airline market, what can we do to make our passengers loyal to us?* Well, the passengers were there, ready and willing to take steps toward love in their hearts for the airline, and then the airline, ignorant of the most powerful force in business, stopped them dead.

Acting lovelessly, they snuffed out the very thing they wanted the most.

## 2. Harmony

### "Do you know what I'm feeling, and do you care?"

The next feeling on your journey toward love in your heart is *harmony*.

Some nurses can give virtually painless injections.

It's true. The last time you went to the doctor with pain of some kind, you were asked this question, weren't you? "On a scale of 1–10, with 10 high, how would you rate your pain right now?" When I studied the top-performing nurses, as defined by the commonsense criteria of "nurses you want to hire more like," I discovered that these nurses, when giving an injection or inserting an IV, received consistently lower pain ratings from their patients.

I wondered what these pain-reducing nurses were doing. Was it a softer swabbing technique, or a specific needle angle? Or were they masters of distraction, always ready with a well-timed joke to divert the patient's attention from the painful prick?

None of the above, it turns out. Some swabbed gently, some were firm. And sure, some were smiley and lighthearted, but other equally great nurses were pragmatic and businesslike in their approach to patients.

The difference, it turned out, the thing that truly separated the great nurses from all the rest, was what they said right before they plunged the needle in. The best nurses said some version of "This is going to hurt a little bit. I'll try to make it hurt as little as possible." They knew the patient was fearful, that anticipating the pain was worse even than the pain itself. But rather than ignoring their fear, or trying to distract the patient from it, or even dismissing it, instead they called them out. They explicitly met the patient right where they were at emotionally—"This is going to hurt a little bit"—and in so doing, the patient came to feel as though the pain was lessened. The best nurses positioned themselves as being in emotional harmony with their patients. They "shared" their patients' pain. So much so that the patients, measurably, recorded lower levels of pain.

If I want you, my patient, to be drawn into my world, to keep tying your identity so closely to your experience that you tell your loved ones about it, then I need to do everything I can to meet you where you're at emotionally. I need to make you feel emotional *harmony*.

Even if I want to move you to a different emotional state—I am the nurse who wants you to feel protected and cared for; I am the customer service person who wants to correct the error; I am the manager who wants to turn my team's anxiety into confidence—I can do this only if I show you I'm aware of your current emotional state. I can move you only if I meet you.

Life is discordant. Each person moves through it knowing they will have to switch from an email requiring an analytical response, to a text from a loved one needing reassurance, to a bill needing to be paid, to a friend asking advice, all while jostling with the other passengers of the train they just boarded, digging their ticket out from some pocket or app, and then turning off their phone with the text from their mom unanswered.

Life is constant emotional code-switching. And as meta-analytic data shows, code-switching and multitasking are deeply stressful for us humans. Both require the person either to jump—mentally and emotionally—from one state to another or to maintain constantly two or more personas so each can be activated at a moment's notice.

If I want to treat you lovingly, I'll think about how to free you from this torrent of emotional incoherence and the stress it brings. I'll anticipate what emotional state you're in, and carefully give you cues to honor this state: "This is going to hurt. I'll try to make it hurt as little as I can." And in so doing, I'll draw you further and further into my world.

On the flip side, if I approach you with the wrong tone, even though you might not be able to articulate it, it will jar you. You'll recoil, lean out, and start to close yourself off from me. Your psychological journey toward love in your heart will stall.

Or worse, my tone will be so disharmonious, so out of touch with your emotional state, that you'll actually turn around and walk away from me.

Last month the lease on my Audi was up, and like many leaseholders, I was starting to get excited about which car I might lease next. Another Audi was certainly in the mix. I've leased a few Audis over the years, and their new models were enticing. But then I received a call from Audi. A robocall. A female voice that I knew was artificial. "This is Audi calling," she said. "The lease on your Audi A3 is ending. You have failed to schedule your termination inspection."

I've failed? My termination inspection? I had no idea what this was, but it sounded bad. Like I'd done something wrong. So I ignored it. And then, over the subsequent three weeks, I received three more robocalls, each one intoning ominously that I needed to "schedule my termination inspection."

These calls weren't a negative experience, per se. They were just emotionally jarring. Like millions of other leaseholders coming to the end of their car lease, I was jazzed, excited, little bursts of dopamine pinging me as I scrolled through the pictures of the latest models. And then Audi hit me with "You've failed to schedule your termination inspection."

So I rocked back on my emotional heels. I leaned out. And I kept leaning out, until I got to the end of my lease, and turned my back on Audi—not forever, perhaps, but at least for the next five years.

This sort of thing happens all the time. Leaders ignore the human's emotional state, and so design their touchpoints for efficiency rather than harmony. Think back to those employees calling their company to ask a question about their health insurance or their ability to set up family leave. Their emotional state is fraught, anxious: when we call about these sorts of health-related matters, we are taut with tension, hoping that we're going to be in safe and loving hands. And what do virtually all companies do, no matter their size? They outsource insurance and family leave services to a third-party provider because it's the cost-effective thing to do. And so these employees, in their fraught state, are handed off to some provider call center in the suburbs of Phoenix or San Antonio, where the person who answers their call has little understanding or empathy for their situation, and whose first question is: "What's your employee number?"

Then these companies wonder why their talent brand is so fragile, why employees are threatening to strike, and why they have such high levels of employee turnover.

By designing efficient but unloving touchpoints they've unwittingly brought disharmony into their employees' experience—and then these employees have turned around, psychologically or physically, and walked right out the door.

## 3. Significance

### "Do you know my story, and do you care?"

When we love someone, we offer them the feeling of *significance*, of being seen as an individual.

No one is under the illusion that the world sees who they truly are. Instead, while each person feels with intense vividness their own loves, loathes, joys, fears, goals, disappointments, insights, and frustrations, they also realize that the world is blind to all this. (Well, most people do!)

And this friction is ongoingly stressful. Life is an unending series of friction-filled moments in which each person struggles to reconcile how precious and important their own unique life feels to them, with the world's seeming indifference to it.

When you walk into the doctor's office, you are not so self-involved to think that none of the rules apply to you: indeed, as part of giving you a feeling of *control* I may have already told you the "rules" of my world, such as how to book an appointment, or how to reach me directly, and these rules have given you agency. They've made my world operationally simple for you. Counterintuitively, knowing *my* rules gives *you* control.

However, you still walk into my world believing in every fiber that you are a special case. If I want you to continue your journey toward tying your identity to mine so tightly that you say, "I love my doc!" then I'll find a way to honor your need to feel significant. I'll get you to feel that, with me, *one size fits one.*

During research into the very best doctors, I would ask them a simple question: "What is the best way to put a patient at ease?" You can imagine all the possible range of answers I'd hear. Everything from "Always just stick to the facts" to "Never sit behind your desk" to "Prominently display your board certifications."

And yet this is not what the best doctors said. They all said the same thing. Which was the same answer, as it happens, when, during research into great teachers, I'd asked them: "What is the best way to help a student learn?"

And the same answer, when I'd interviewed excellent team leaders and asked: "What is the best way to motivate a team member?"

All these excellent practitioners of their craft, these 5s, when asked to pinpoint the best practice for getting the outcomes they want, said this: "It depends."

And more specifically, "It depends on the patient, the student, the team member." The very best at anything involving other humans live in a world of "It depends." They know that each person is not only wired a little differently, but also has had different experiences, and, in the case of a doctor's patients, has a different genome.

A world of "It depends" is a world sensitive to the idiosyncrasies of each person. It is a world where the doctor, the teacher, the manager, asks lots of open-ended questions and then keeps quiet. A world of curiosity to the lived reality of each person, where the expectation is that this lived reality is true and worth listening to, and where doing right by the other person means "right for them," not "right universally." It is a loving world.

If I show you that I am attentive to your unique story, if I design systems that enable me to capture and recall this story, and if I tell you what exceptions I can make based on this story, you will keep leaning into your journey toward me. With each detail of your life played back to you, you will take one more step closer to interlacing your identity with the experiences I've given you, one step closer toward saying "Yes, I loved that!"

## 4. The Warmth of Others

### "Who's with me, and how can they help?"

When we treat someone lovingly we offer them the *warmth of others.*

The world is atomized, and increasingly so. All the meta-analytic data points to the fact that when a human feels disconnected from other humans, all manner of negative outcomes occur. Health outcomes suffer when people feel lonely. More workdays are missed and more accidents on the job occur when workers feel disconnected from their teammates. Students, separated from one another during the pandemic, experienced poorer learning outcomes and higher levels of stress and mental illness. Customers buy less and consume less when they don't feel connected to, and reinforced by, the sight of people like them.

These discoveries are well known, so it's surprising how little attention is paid to making each customer, employee, student, and patient feel connected to others.

Take those handoffs as one example. When you walk into the doctor's office you are looking for the warmth of an "other" to be your guide into my world. Instinctively you know you're going to get lost, and so from the first moment you enter the waiting room, you're wondering which other human is going to see you lost, and show you how to keep moving forward. Someone (1) who will show you how to gain control in this world, (2) who will use the right words and the right tone to meet you where you're at emotionally, and (3) who will see you as a unique individual and so give you that gloriously human feeling of significance. Who will be your guide?

And yet, sitting there in your waiting room, you see no guide. You see a receptionist, who may be welcoming and kind, but who then begins the series of handoffs, to the scheduler, the first nurse, the second, then me, then the nurse again, then the billing person, then back to the scheduler to set up your next visit.

These handoffs work for me, but not for you. Each one stalls your journey toward love. You are looking for the warmth of others. You are looking for some other human who can reassure you that you are seen, and heard, and helped. And each handoff increases your stress that you are going through this experience alone. Each handoff forces you to question whether this new person understands the control you need, or senses how you're feeling, or recognizes how special your special case is.

Of course, you don't expect me, your doctor, to take care of all these touchpoints—I'm busy. You get that. It's one of the rules of my world that I can't hold every patient's hand all the time. Fine. But nonetheless you do expect me to be aware that each handoff is unloving, and to figure out some emotionally intelligent way to inject loving back into your experience.

For example, and first, can I reduce the number of handoffs? And second, if I've truly got it down to the barest minimum, can I figure out a way to reassure you that whichever new other you are about to be handed off to knows your emotional state and the uniqueness of your situation? "Please," you say quietly, "manage my handoffs in an intentionally loving way."

There are, of course, other others whose warmth you would dearly love to feel. If you join a company as a new recruit, can they deliberately connect you with a cohort with whom you can share your journey? If you buy a new car, are there other owners of this car to whom you might be introduced to reinforce your enthusiasm and answer your questions? If you buy a cool new toothpaste brand, can they show you some cool new user-generated content that reassures you that there are other people like you who are ditching their old toothpaste and branching out into something new?

Yes, there are lots of potential others you could be connected to. But best to start simple. The first other you're looking for is a single point of contact guide. If I serve you up one of those you'll feel held, safe, cared for, and you'll keep advancing toward me with confidence, moving ever closer to that feeling of love in your heart for the experience I'm giving you.

But if I ignore your need for the warmth of others, if I look past your need for a loving guide, if I subject you to one loveless handoff after another, then you'll stiffen, recoil, and step back and away. And you'll never become a messenger of love for me, or my company, or my brand. You'll devolve into being merely a check, a bill, a table to be turned, a patient to be invoiced, a car buyer to be processed. Because I saw you as this, and acted as though this was all you were, you became it.

## 5. Growth

### "How will I be more capable tomorrow?"

One of the strangest sights in business is the sheer number of ex-employees that Lululemon has spotlighted in their stores. Large black-and-white photos hanging on the wall. Walk into your local Lulu, or visit their website, and you'll see scores of them. The subject of each one is a person in Lulu gear doing some kind of physical activity. These are Lululemon ambassadors, folks from the community whose presence on the walls is meant to convey to customers that *We know you. We are part of your world. When you buy from us you're not just buying a product, you're joining a group of people who share your values.*

On one level this serves as a good example of the company offering its customers the warmth of others. But on another level, what's most interesting about these photos is that so many of them depict people who used to work in Lululemon's stores but who have since moved on. To start their own yoga studio, or become a personal trainer, or design their own running shoes.

Can you think of any other company doing this? Celebrating people who have left the company. My experience of the corporate world is that, when an employee leaves, most companies act as if the person never existed. Their names are rarely brought up in meetings, and their contributions, whatever they may have been, are quickly submerged and subsumed into the broader company's efforts.

Lululemon has taken a radically different approach. When a new person joins the company they are asked their goals, and if someone shares that at some point they want to open their own yoga studio, the company commits to helping them make that happen. Their stance toward their people is that each person is a work-in-progress, and that the role of Lululemon should be to become part of each's person's progress. This part might be two years, five years, or twenty years, but no matter how long it lasts, Lululemon's part is simply to be a means to fuel their people's growth. They spotlight ex-employees to celebrate this *growth*.

This is a deeply loving thing to do. Love is a forward-facing emotion. When we love someone we show them that we are always thinking about their future and how we can help make it better for them. We imagine how their relationship with us might help them grow, and in what specific ways they might grow, and we intentionally create systems and processes to facilitate this growth. When we love someone we are always thinking about what they might need from us next.

And the human on the receiving end feels more bonded to us. Humans are conscious that time's arrow points ever forward, and that tomorrow they'll need to be ready and equipped to handle whatever life throws their way. Stressed by the challenges of an ever-changing world, we develop deep emotional attachment to any person or place that helps us get bigger. This is why the strongest alumni associations in the world are connected to colleges and to the armed forces. Both institutions are expressly committed to helping people become bigger—better equipped, more highly trained, more powerfully credentialed. When we leave these places, we're conscious of how much of them we take with us, and our loyalty to them grows. Love, learning, and loyalty are all tightly linked.

So, if I, your doctor, want to strengthen your loyalty to me—indeed, if any organization wants to create more loyalty among customers and employees—I'll view each touchpoint as an opportunity to better equip you for tomorrow. Even the smallest interaction is a chance for you to learn something. Can my receptionist give you a hack for the best way to reach me to ask post-visit advice? Can I hang a poster in the waiting room with the best dietary advice, a "little known fact" about exercise, or a simple routine for getting a better night's rest? Or perhaps I could include on every prescription one individualized action item that will help you grow just a little healthier before your next visit.

When you look at humans as a work in progress, as an organism primed to become bonded to those who help them grow, you realize just how many learning opportunities exist—and are so often missed.

All workers receive a paycheck: this paycheck, whether physical or digital, is a communication device, so wouldn't it be valuable to include on each check one small piece of advice on financial fluency?

Cars are becoming increasingly technologically complex: Who among us car buyers wouldn't want to have just a little bit of learning about how to work our vehicle and get it synced up with the other gadgets in our life?

Airline seat prices are absurdly unpredictable, and loyalty programs are graduate-level complex, so who wouldn't want their airline to figure out a few simple ways to explain how to be the smartest passenger possible?

Companies don't take advantage of teaching touchpoints such as these not because it's too costly, but because they don't appreciate the link between love, learning, and loyalty. Unaware of the singular power of love to drive productive behaviors, they haven't studied it closely, and so haven't realized how simple, easy, and hugely valuable it would be to lean into humans' craving for learning. Blind to love, they fail to teach.

The best companies and the wisest leaders won't make this mistake. They'll keep their eyes open to the power of love and will be relentless in looking for ways to treat people lovingly.

. . .

These five feelings (figure 3-1) are your blueprint for designing love in to the lives of others. You, the DLI leader, have the power to give people a feeling of control. Power to create feelings of harmony. Power to make them feel significant. Power to surround them with the warmth of others. Power to help them grow.

By focusing your power on these five feelings, you can design love in to all manner of experiences. You can build recruiting programs that draw in the best people and then keep them loving you and loving the team they joined. You can build teams of teams of teams with love in each of them, and so make a truly loving company, the kind that flourishes because each associate is flourishing. You can build services and products that draw in a growing flood of customers who stay longer, spend more and are happy to, and who then turn around and advocate you to friends and family.

Before we dive deeper into precisely how, let's use the sequence of these five feelings to pull back the curtain and see what they reveal about how certain aspects of the world actually work.

FIGURE 3-1

**The five feelings of love**

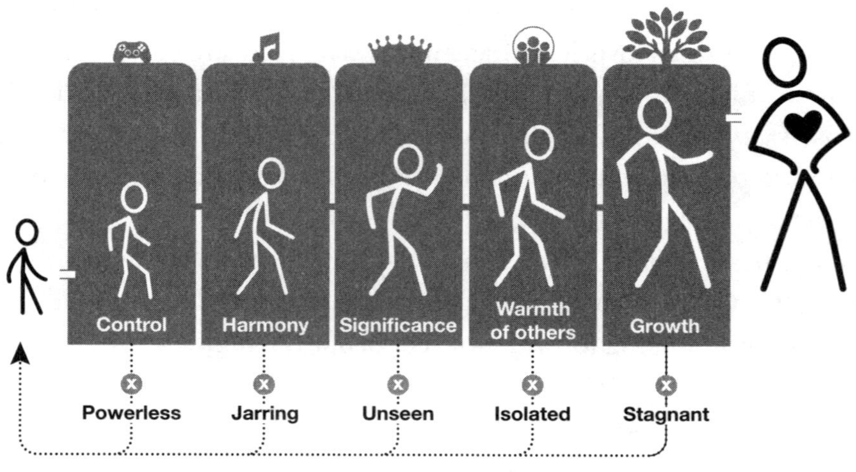

## The Sequence Matters

### "Love builds. Or it isn't love."

This may not be high on your list of fun excursions, but consider for a moment a typical visit to the Department of Motor Vehicles:

> Walking in it's not immediately clear which line you should stand in or how long it's going to take, and when you do eventually make it to the counter you cede any control to the bureaucratic processes you're about to be subject to—so, you're *powerless*.
>
> There is no signage, no language, and with very rare exceptions, no people showing you that your current feelings are taken into consideration—so, it's *jarring*.
>
> Your unique situation is irrelevant to the standard DMV processes—so, you feel *unseen*.
>
> Whom you are with, or who might be going through these processes with you, is never brought up—so, you're *isolated*.
>
> But at least you might walk out of there having received your driver's license, and therefore you might feel bigger and better equipped to face tomorrow—so, yes, there may be some *growth*.

Without question there's more government agencies could do to design love in to the experiences they're making—if they're so inclined. But the fact that we loathe going to the DMV, even though there's a chance we might feel a bit bigger at the end of it, goes to show how important the sequence of those five feelings is to creating genuine love. At the DMV, your growth at the end of the experience doesn't make up for the lovelessness of getting there.

The same applies to all experiences you, the leader, create, whether for customers or employees. Sequence matters. And when you get the sequence wrong, or when you're blind to the need to sequence experiences, your best-laid and truly well-intended plans falter.

The other day a company asked me to speak at one of those high-end spa-resort places—Miravel, Austin—the kind where you have to book your daily schedule in advance, a schedule that might include standard fare such as Hot Yoga at 8 a.m., and a hike at 9, but by the afternoon you might find yourself signed up for Equine Therapy at 2, followed by BOSU Balance Challenge (don't ask, no idea) or Floating Meditation (also no idea) at 4.

Anyway, it was all very high-end, and most of the clientele matched the experience. With one exception. Or one group of exceptions. Every third person at the health-food restaurant, or standing next to you at Kundalini Yoga, or floating by you during meditation, was a twenty-seven-year-old. There or thereabouts. Lots of late-twenties young professionals, of varying races, genders, and yoga mastery, and clearly there without parents or families. They didn't seem to know each other, but were nonetheless all of a piece, like extras in the same movie.

Eventually, as we were walking with a couple of them down to Beekeeping for Beginners, I summoned up the impoliteness to ask: "Excuse me, but what the heck are you all doing here?"

It turned out they all worked for a large professional services firm. Apparently this firm, like all professional services firms, was struggling not only to recruit top talent from the best schools, but also to hold on to that talent long enough to make the recruiting investment of time and money pay off. And so one of the tactics they'd landed on was to lure all new recruits with a promise that, no matter where you worked in the firm, if you stayed either three years, or until you were promoted to senior manager, you would be rewarded with an all-expenses-paid trip to the Miravel Resort of your choosing.

So this explained why they all "felt" the same, yet didn't actually know each other.

"Does it work?" I asked. "Do you all stick around?"

"Oh yes, the Miravel trip is what we all stay for! They tell us about it when we're first recruited, and you can hear the stories of how great it is all around the company."

"And then what?" I asked. "After you come back from the trip?"

"Oh, then we're free to go."

Then they're "free to go"? Like prisoners?

It was a strange word choice. And one we heard from all the other firm employees we came to talk to during our stay. The Miravel trip was much appreciated by them, and definitely "worked" in the transactional sense that it coerced them into not leaving until after the trip. But it didn't do anything more. It didn't create in them any deeper feelings of connection, or goodwill, or loyalty to the firm. It didn't make them love their company.

This professional services firm was trying to build love backward. The Miravel trip promised their young employees growth, and perhaps, as they all met and formed acquaintanceships on paddle-boarding or hatchet-throwing sessions, a little warmth of others.

But love doesn't work this way. Love builds in sequence and over time, one touchpoint after another. If you don't start by designing control into the experience, and then drawing the person in with emotional harmony, and offering them a feeling of personal significance, the final two feelings—warmth of others and growth—don't register. They have nothing to connect to, no foundation. And when love's foundation is missing, we humans sense it, and we lean way the heck out. We don't trust it. It's unsafe.

This firm, with the very best of intentions, had tried a shortcut to creating love in the hearts of their employees. And with love there are no shortcuts.

## True Love Requires All Five Feelings

### "Why do we love to hate social media?"

Back in 2020 Ed Sheeran announced he was taking a break from social media—and we all admired him for it.

In 2022 Tom Holland of *Spiderman* fame revealed that he had done the same, for his "mental health"—and again, we all nodded our heads in approval. Well done, Tom, for taking care of your mental well-being. Well done for doing something that many of us aspire to do, but don't.

What is it with social media? Why do we have this hate/love relationship with it? We are drawn in to it—well, hundreds of millions of us are—and yet we are clearly ambivalent about it. We grab our phone to check it the moment we wake up, and yet we applaud celebrities for their moral virtue when they give it up. What's going on?

Well, don't be too hard on yourself. Yes, it has a hold on you, but so it does for almost all of us. The five feelings can help explain why you find it simultaneously so enticing and so empty. Its first promise to you is control. All the biggest social media apps—Instagram, TikTok, Snapchat—tell you clearly what their world is all about, and make it so very easy for you to take action in this world. To post your pics, videos, and stories; edit them; and then, one click, and all your contacts are there to share it with. Since everything is user-generated content, social media is laser-focused on giving the user immediate control.

And then of course, there are the reactions. The world of social media is rich with signs of emotional harmony. Not only do you get tons of feedback reinforcing your emotional state—*You love moving to Portugal? Me too! Your dog is a drama queen? How funny, mine too!*—but soon your feeds get pumped full of content all designed to meet you right where you're at. And these feeds have no intention of moving you anywhere. They're happy just to keep reinforcing the harmony of your emotions through the content you're consuming.

And significance? Oh yes, the specifics of your unique life, loves, loathes, and experiences, you get to share all of those.

> *My Beige Flag is my boyfriend never putting the top back on the ketchup bottle.*
>
> *Oh really, mine is the same, but ever so slightly different: mine is that he doesn't put the top back on the mayo jar.*

*Your Roman Empire is Uno cards from the 1930s? Interesting. Mine is Taylor Swift lyrics featuring the word "mall."*

You get to present, in increasingly minor detail, the specifics of your unique persona. And each post reinforces your feeling of specialness, of significance.

One feeling after another, social media plays perfectly to your human craving for the sequence of loving experiences, *control* to *harmony* to *significance*, drawing you in further and further, like water to a drain.

But here's the question: If they've got lots of love right, why do we all hate it so much? Or, flipped around, why do we hate ourselves for loving it?

Through the five-feelings sequence we can see one reason why. Because social media offers only the first blush of love. On social media we find *control* and *harmony* and *significance*—but no *warmth of others*, and no *growth*.

Yes, we encounter "others" on social media, but these others don't know us. They don't want to do all they can to help us flourish. They're just there. Watching, commenting, lurking. They're not warm. They're just others. Which is why the world of social media is so lonely.

And growth? No, not really. You grow your followers on social media, but not much else. Nothing in these apps genuinely wants to help you feel more capable tomorrow. None of them will be there for you tomorrow. Occasionally you might bump into a thought-provoking post on nutrition, say, or some therapeutic opinion, and these might give you a feeling of control, as all useful information does. But on some level you know that no matter how well-intended the poster is, they are United Airlines, trying to grab, hold onto, and monetize your eyeballs. They don't know you. They aren't truly invested in your growth. They know your click rate on their link, or their code, or whatever, and that's what they focus on.

Nothing about social media expresses a "deep and unwavering commitment to your flourishing." It's the siren song luring you in with the first three notes of love—*control, harmony, significance*—and then casting you off to thrash about in the froth of fake "others" and false "growth" until, like so many of us, you smash onto the rocks.

So, let's all say it: social media is unloving. It doesn't care about your flourishing, and it never will. If you want to devote your human time and energy to it, then go for it. But please don't expect your time and energy ever to lead to extreme positive outcomes for you. Social media will always leave you a little smaller than you were before. It's designed that way.

Keep your critical thinking alert to *any* experience that has targeted the first couple of feelings and then ignored the rest. As social media does, these experiences draw you in, even as they drain you of power. The DLI leader recognizes this, and refuses to be drawn in.

## What's the Opposite of Lovingly?

### "No love for legal."

Take a look again at those five feelings, and reflect on what their opposite is. I've used the words *helpless, jarring, unseen, isolated,* and *stagnant*. Perhaps you would use different words, but if you think for a minute about which institutions, organizations, or groups treat you this way, which come to mind?

Here's one: lawyers. Seen through the filter of these five feelings the opposite of *lovingly* isn't *unlovingly*. It's *legally*.

When we make doing something legally the priority, we are, if we're not extraordinarily careful, draining love from the experience:

1. We are making sure that each person is subject to the force of the law—so, no *control*.

2. Their emotions are irrelevant—no *harmony*.
3. The law is blind to their "unique story"—no *significance*.
4. They are separated from others in being judged by the law—no *warmth of others*.
5. Their future actions and growth are never considered—so, no *growth*.

No one should blame lawyers for this approach: Lady Justice is blindfolded for good reason. What should matter to each of us is that we are living in an increasingly legalistic world, where each customer/company transaction has to be "run through legal," where many HR departments report up through legal—their role is more and more to protect the company from us, the employees—and where we employees are increasingly empowered through federal and state legislation to use the law to protect our employment rights.

This means that a growing proportion of the relationship between customer and company, employer and employee, is being played out in the context of a legal framework. Which means an unloving framework.

The law is best fit for defining the boundaries of a relationship; it is a poor fit for defining the ingredients of the relationship. The more it does so, the more organizations allow legal considerations to dominate the conversation, to dictate the interactions of our working relationships, the more they will drive out love. When legal wins, love withers.

The rise of the general counsel (GC) is one of the more worrying signs of what's happening in the world of work. Be wary of any company that moves its GC into top leadership roles. Of course there will be exceptions—general counsels who have climbed above the legal scaffolding to see, and delight in, the crowds of weird and wonderful people. But one might predict that, as a rule, a person schooled in and rewarded by legal ways of looking at people will struggle to excel at replacing the word *legal* with the word *loving*. It's not their fault.

But it's worth noting. Before you join any company or organization, look to see how many executive committee (EC) members came up through the legal profession. When you see an EC replete with lawyers, it might be light on love.

These five feelings and their sequence serve as your filter for revealing experiences where love has been designed out—and your playbook for how to design love in.

In the next chapters we'll put this playbook into practice.

Part Two

# HOW TO DESIGN LOVE IN AS A LEADER

# 4

# Design Love In for Your Team

You might think that the best leaders possess a long list of competencies. Perhaps you've read books detailing these competencies, or perhaps your company measures its leaders against some required list, using 360-degree surveys or performance ratings.

No matter how specific these lists are, or how tightly the ratings are tied to specific behaviors, the overwhelming body of data-based evidence reveals that all of these lists lack validity: we have no reliable way of measuring leader competencies, and so no valid way of proving that the best leaders possess more of them than average leaders.

The fact is, the best leaders do not have much in common at all. They do not all possess the same list of competencies. Nor do these leaders get better by identifying and then trying to acquire the competencies on the list that they lack.

Yes, it might be desirable for a leader to possess strategic thinking or executive presence or emotional intelligence, but the data shows that all of these skills are simply nice-to-haves. For every leader who excels at strategic thinking, you find a different excellent leader whose influence comes from their ability to build consensus. Another leads through salesmanship. Another is an empath. Another executes with predictability and precision.

All truly influential leaders are different. For every Steve Jobs, there's a Warren Buffett. For every Barack Obama, there's a Margaret Thatcher. For every Elon Musk, there's a Greta Thunberg. Think of the very best leaders you know. Line them up in your mind. Visualize how they led, the moves they made, their tone of voice, their passions, their concerns, the level of their intensity, their intelligence, their creativity. They were all so different, weren't they? Virtually nothing in common at all.

Look closely at excellent leaders and you realize that, in the real world, they all shared only one thing: followers. Though each possessed their own style and was animated by different missions and goals, they all excelled at getting others to follow them. These leaders all did some specific things that touched the hearts of other people—so much so that these people became followers and were prepared to go through hell and high water to help the leader make real their vision of a better world.

And these "things" are, simply put, experiences. Leaders make experiences for their followers, and these experiences drive behaviors that drive outcomes. These leaders are not strategists, or analysts, or planners, or team builders, or salespeople. Well, they may be all of these things. They may even excel at some of these. But a person can excel at all of them and still struggle as a leader.

The only surefire way to excel as a leader is to excel as a maker of experiences for your people. Create extreme positive experiences for your people, and you will create extreme positive behaviors: you will get all their "discretionary effort," you will see them at their very best. Ignore your role as an experience-maker and you'll get the minimum behaviors, the phone-it-in behaviors, the ROAD warrior behaviors (Retired While on Active Duty.)

Experience-making. It's your fundamental job as a leader.

Of course, this is not to say that you can't lead people using power from other sources. You can get power from your position, or your title, or your ability to control budgets or timelines or permissions. And, using this power, you can coerce people into behaving in a certain way. But this sort of coercion, while it can affect people's behavior, and while it can sometimes be mistaken for leadership, never leads to sustained excellence.

To achieve sustained excellence requires that your people, your followers, are themselves *choosing* to behave in certain ways. Giving their maximum is a choice. And the only way for you to get this from your people is to design for them the kinds of experiences that they want to step into. Your true power as a leader comes from your ability to create those five feelings in others.

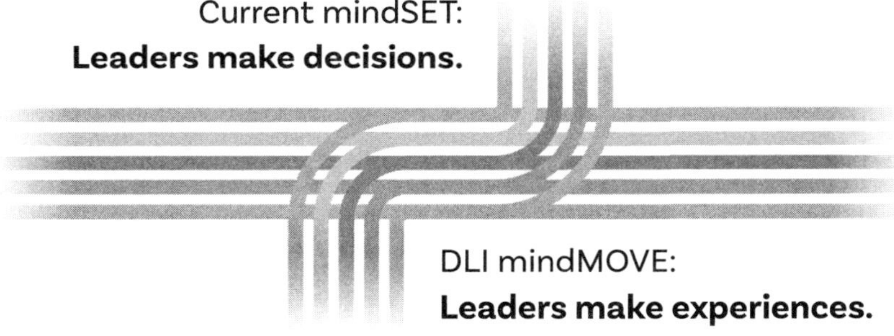


## How to Lead Your Team with Love

We now know that the kind of experiences that lead people to perform at their best are genuinely loving experiences, with this as our definition of loving: *the deep and unwavering commitment to the flourishing of a human.*

In theory this can seem like a heavy lift: *Who has the time to be deep and unwavering about anything?!* But in practice, this feeling of love-in-my-heart for my leader, or love-in-my-heart for my team, grows over time. It doesn't require an outlandish display of altruism or self-sacrifice on the part of you, the leader. All it requires is the intelligent design of daily and weekly experiences.

You don't need anyone else's permission to make these experiences for your people. You can use the five feelings as a channel for your own power, and find *your* way of helping your team feel them.

And in doing so, you can lead with love.

To help you excel at this, let's start with the foundation, the ABCs if you will, of experience-making, and then we'll use the five feelings to get even more precise.

A: Your Authenticity

B: Your Beliefs

C: Your Customs

## A: Your Authenticity

The most interesting discovery from the last twenty-five years of measuring the strengths of leaders and then correlating the results to the leader's team engagement scores is that the leaders with the strongest strengths produced the most engaged teams. This does not mean that these leaders all possessed the same combination of strengths; they most certainly did not. What it means, instead, is that the leaders with the most *defined* combination of strengths were the most successful in engaging their people.

And it didn't seem to matter which combination of strengths they possessed. In StrengthsFinder language it might have been Futuristic and Command, or Intellection and Relator, or Input and Focus. In StandOut language it might have been Equalizer/Adviser, or my personal top two Stimulator/Creator. What mattered in terms of driving high engagement scores was not the combination. It was the *definition* of the combination. That is, what mattered wasn't which strengths the leader had; it was how much of them they had. If the leader had a lot—as measured by either StrengthsFinder or StandOut—then the team engagement scores were likely to be much higher.

This research finding confirms what you have probably long believed about the best leaders: you neither want nor expect them to be perfect. But you do want them to be authentic. Authenticity in the leader breeds confidence in the followers. Because authenticity is the cousin of predictability. And predictability is the foundation of followership.

You are trying, as all leaders do, to rally me and my teammates to create a better future. You're excited about this better future and you keep telling me and my teammates how excited we should be too. Your problem is that the future is unknown, and I and my teammates are fearful of the unknown. It makes us anxious. Which is not such a daft thing to be. The future is around a corner we cannot see, and so to be a little cautious, a little deliberative about following you around this corner is an adaptive human response: those humans who bounded around the corner wide-eyed and credulous often didn't live long enough to pass on their genes.

Your challenge, therefore, is to take our natural and adaptive fear of the unknown and turn it into confidence. Into a spirited and enthusiastic following of you around the corner and into the future. Faced with this alchemy—turning anxiety into confidence—the most powerful tool in your belt is yourself. And specifically, your conscious understanding of yourself—what you love, what you loathe, and how to turn the former into contribution.

As the engagement data shows, we do *not* care about the specifics of what you love. We care only that you know what you love, and that you have figured out how to express it intelligently. We might not have the same loves as you. We might not even agree with precisely how you express yours. What we want most of all from you is clear and consistent expression of them. And we want this because it makes you more *predictable.* If we are to follow you enthusiastically around the corner, it helps our confidence mightily if we can predict how you are going to behave once around the corner. There's a lot we don't know. Please, we ask, remove one of the unknowns by being a leader whose loves are on consistent and vivid display, every single day.

You might be the kind of leader who loves to see the data before making a decision. Fine, then tell us that, and behave consistently with that.

You might be the kind of leader who craves consensus before forging ahead. Again, fine. Just be sure to tell us this is how you operate, and keep unapologetically behaving in line with that.

You might be a what-if thinking leader. Or an assertive leader. Or a ruminative leader, requiring loads of time to ponder and noodle.

These are all fine with us. These all work. Just make sure that you know who the heck you are, and ideally you tell us—and keep telling us—that you know who you are and how you operate in the world. The clearer you are with us about what you love the fewer uncertainties we'll have to deal with as we summon up the courage to follow you into the future.

This is the Mover role in action—namely, the ability to move through the activities and demands of each day and draw the energy you need to keep moving; to be invigorated by your days rather than drained by them. This Mover role was the focus of my previous book *Love + Work,* which introduced the concept of "red threads." The metaphor being that, each day, your life is showing you many thousands of different threads—different activities, moments, situations, interactions. These "threads" make up the fabric of your day. Many of them are emotionally neutral—threads that are black, white, gray, green. Stuff you have to do, to push through, and cross off your list.

But some of these threads are red. These red threads are those things you love—activities you find yourself looking forward to, interactions where you feel in control, moments when time flies by, even places or spaces in your home when you feel most yourself. (I've included a Red Questionnaire at DesignLoveIn.com to help you become increasingly precise in pinpointing your red threads.)

What's important now is *not* that you fill your entire life with red threads: in fact, there's data out of the Mayo Clinic that suggests that the most successful people require their life to contain a threshold of only 20 percent red threads every day.

What's important is that you learn how to weave these threads in to your days. To turn what you love into meaningful contribution. To take these threads and, with intelligence and an open heart, design love in to your own life. As a DLI leader, you do not need to find a job you love. But, for all our sakes—yours and ours—you do need to find the love in what you do.

And please don't worry about loving an activity too much, or having too much of certain strengths. There is no data anywhere that shows that leaders who correctly pinpoint what they have too much of, and succeed in reducing it, are more successful at getting people to follow them. None. Anywhere. The myth of "your strengths turn into weaknesses when you have too much of them" is precisely that: a myth.

You can never love something too much: as the research reveals, the more vivid your loves are, the more engagement you'll create in your people. What we can say is that while you can't have too much, you can channel what you love intelligently, or unintelligently. You can turn what you love into contribution effectively or ineffectively. And so, it is on you—once you've pinpointed your red threads as a leader—to express them as intelligently and as effectively as possible.

This means spending some considerable time thinking about what you love most, what your dominant strengths are, and then practicing and refining how all this shows up to your people. Don't lean out. Don't shy away. Don't tone yourself down. Instead, do the opposite. Lean in. Dive into the detail of what you love and find the most intelligent ways to express yourself.

If you are an assertive leader, shouting more, and louder, probably isn't intelligent. Whereas experimenting with the best phrases, and the most effective tones of voice, to confront an issue or a person head-on is very intelligent.

If you are a strategic thinker, try to learn the most compelling way for you to share your natural gift for projection and scenario planning.

If you are a consensus builder, design explicit ways for you to bring your people together, and reassure them that your methods are not a blocker of action, but an important step for you in sustaining action.

Above all, try to be as explicit with us as possible in terms of what you know your loves to be, and how they translate into your day-to-day decisions. Do this well, our confidence will increase and we will reward you with our followership.

## B: Your Beliefs

One of the last pieces of research I did with my mentor Dr. Don Clifton before his passing was a primary qualitative research project on the practices of the most effective leaders. We weren't looking for lists of shared strengths or competencies; our quantitative research had long since revealed the fundamental idiosyncrasy of the best leaders. Instead, we conducted hundreds of focus groups to try to learn if the best leaders shared any actual practices. Not did they possess the same strengths or loves, but instead, did they behave the same?

We found a few, which, after much debate, we wound up calling demands. These were actions that the most effective leaders demanded of themselves.

*Make sense of experience* was one: this was the demand to always evaluate why things played out the way they did to ensure that the leader didn't fall into the comfort of familiarity, and simply repeat the same moves again and again.

*Build knowledge of self* was another one, which speaks directly to the need to pinpoint those red threads.

But at the heart of these demands, one that we heard vividly in the interviews and focus groups, was *share your beliefs*.

One side of this demand was internal—these leaders disciplined themselves to find time during the year to sit with their beliefs and clarify them. Which, when we asked about it, seemed to mean: take time away from the busyness of work, surface their core beliefs—write them down, put them up on the wall on flip charts—and then push on them. *Do I still believe this? Has anything happened recently to challenge or change this belief? Why is this belief still so important to me?* This demand to constantly be clarifying their beliefs undoubtedly gave them an aura of certainty and solidity—which then gave their people more confidence.

The other side of this demand was external—these leaders seemed to understand that the job of a leader was to play to an audience, and they couldn't expect the audience to read their mind, or their heart. And so, they took it upon themselves to share their beliefs with their followers.

This insight is one of the most distinctive differences between the best leaders and the average. The average leader views the world through a primarily functional lens. There is work to be done. Tasks to be completed. Emails to send. Standard operating procedure to follow. And the job of the leader, according to this view, is to make sure that everything works as it should, and that the right people are adding their particular efforts to the workflow at the right time.

In contrast, the best leaders understand that they are on stage every day. And that their job is to plan out their words and their movements on stage so that the audience can come away with a shared understanding of the leader's message.

This might seem obvious—*Of course, the leader is being watched every day!*—but you would be surprised by how many leaders forget this. They get so caught up in their own thinking and decisions that they lose sight of the audience. For these leaders the whole concept of experience-making is lost because they've gotten so far away from thinking about the audience and what sort of experience they are having. And once you've forgotten about the person who's having an experience, well then, what's the point of thinking about how to make a great one? There is none. And so, they don't.

So, for you, please keep your audience in mind all the time. You are standing up there in the lights, playing to a crowd. What you say and how you say it will most definitely have an effect on this crowd—and so the demand you must hold yourself accountable to is: *Have I been intentional in how and what I've shared?*

When it comes to beliefs, the best leaders realize that unless they share their beliefs explicitly with the audience, then there's no reason to think that the audience will figure them out for themselves. Audiences can't read your mind, and they don't have the time or the occasion—or the patience—to piece together your beliefs from the jigsaw puzzle of your actions over time. So, if you are to make a solid and predictable experience for your people, take it upon yourself to share your beliefs with them.

From all of my research it appears that there is no one right way to do this: some leaders write a yearly letter to their people expressing their beliefs; some hold weekly meetings in which they ask their team to share real-world examples of the leader's beliefs in action; some create badges and buttons to celebrate teammates who have lived up to the leader's beliefs; some put up pictures in their office of heroes who embody their beliefs.

The method doesn't matter. What matters is that you, the leader, are explicit about what you believe. Not what the company believes—if your efforts to *share your beliefs* amount to nothing more than pointing to the company values posters on the wall, they will come to naught. Not because the company's beliefs are wrong. But because your public endorsement of the company's beliefs doesn't make an experience for your team—well, it does, but it's not *your* experience. It's not an experience that you made. These are not your words. These are not your beliefs. You're just regurgitating someone else's—and for your team this makes you less coherent, not more; less defined, less specifically you, less predictable. And so less likely to earn your team's confidence to follow you into the future.

So, when you share your beliefs, make sure your team know they're truly yours.

## C: Your Customs

By customs, I mean, your routines, your rituals, those actions you customarily take, those habits you bring in and impose on your team.

And please don't say you don't have any customs. You do: you have certain things you repeatedly do and that your team has come to expect from you. So, the question isn't *Do you have them or not?* The question is *Do you have them intentionally, or accidentally?*

The most effective leaders, focused as they are on experience-making, are quite intentional in using their customs to create a certain kind of experience.

When Michael Eisner took over the CEO role at Disney in the mid-eighties, it became very apparent to him that the essence of Disney—that promise of a magical world when you enter the park gates—had suffered over the previous years.

He did many things to reenergize it—from launching a massive building program to signing off on expansions such as the Disney Cruise Line. But, to my mind, one of the most compelling was a custom he instituted the first year he took the helm: henceforth, he said, all leaders at the director level and above would work the third shift in the parks once a month. The third shift starts at 1 a.m. and runs through to 7 a.m. Go into the parks, Eisner told his team, and clean the parks. Not as a punishment. Not as some form of undercover-boss initiative. But instead to anchor for his team that the Disney experience is first and foremost a magical experience, and magic is clean. If the parks are messy, the magic is gone.

Look around at the leaders you admire and I'm sure you'll spot certain customs they established to lock in a certain sort of experience for their team.

Jeff Bezos famously instituted his six-page-memo custom, requiring that anyone who wanted to introduce an idea in a meeting must first produce a six-page memo outlining the idea and its pros and cons. Bezos wanted to create an experience for his team that emphasized the importance of careful and rigorous thought—including customer obsession and long-term horizons—both of which demanded time to think things through, and so the six-page-memo custom become a symbol of how he wanted his people to approach the business.

In direct contrast, one of Jensen Huang's explicit customs is that he never meets one-on-one with his people, and he refuses to read long emails. He calls it the "TL;DR" convention. Which, as you no doubt know, stands for "too long; didn't read."

Huang's entire approach to chip development at Nvidia has been built on fast prototyping, relying on software patches to navigate around bugs in chips, rather than wasting time doing extensive testing of the chips before shipping them to customers. It was this fast prototyping approach that, some say, enabled him to break free of the stranglehold Intel had on the chip market, and establish an ecosystem of customers and suppliers and developers—an ecosystem that Huang was happy to "break" every six months with the introduction of a new chip architecture or configuration.

With speed and agility as his watchword, his TL;DR custom helps create the sort of experience for his team that reinforces his belief in speed and disruption. (Whether this custom works for his direct reports is another matter, which we'll examine later.)

You will want to establish your own customs. Which meetings are sacrosanct to you? How do you run these meetings? What tone are your emails always in? What new customs do you always establish when you take over a new team? Why? Have you explained your customs as clearly and as vividly as Eisner, Bezos, and Huang did?

Again, to be clear, the point here is not that theirs are correct and should be copied. The point is that theirs are vivid, and yours should be too.

Those are the ABCs of experience-making for you and your team. They are your foundation: be authentic with your team about what you love; share with them your core beliefs; and show them which customs you're committed to.

Do this intentionally and you will give us—your team—the stage we need to deliver our very best performances.

. . .

## "I couldn't stop myself."

We are all standing at the entrance to Main Street.

It's Disneyland's seventieth birthday.

Seventy years since Walt Disney opened the park with "Disneyland is your land."

Ten thousand cast members, who've been lining Main Street since the party started at 4:30 a.m., are now crowded in a huge circle around Bob Iger and Josh D'Amaro, as both leaders prepare to make a few remarks to the assembled throng. A select cluster of a thousand guests who've been allowed in to witness up close this birthday celebration are being arranged around the stage. Behind us, in the esplanade separating Disneyland from California Adventure, tens of thousands of guests press forward, pushing for the gates to open.

Josh is the Josh we met in the introduction.

He is today the chairman of Disney Experiences. He started as a low-level finance hire, working somewhere in the bowels of The Walt Disney Company. Today, he's the chairman of the parks, the hotels, the cruise lines, the consumer products divisions, and all of Imagineering. He is, in Disney's world, a big deal. And today, his big deal-ness means he's about to stand on the stage with Bob Iger and welcome guests into the park on Disneyland's birthday.

Except that right now, we can't find him. The stage is set. The lighting is framed. The gates are full to bursting. The train is loaded up with Snow White, Sleeping Beauty, Chip 'n' Dale, and a squad of storm troopers.

Where's Josh?

I'm standing in back of the lighting and cameras and suddenly I spot him. He's behind me. He's snuck out of the choregraphed, well-lit stage enclave and is now out among us. He's made a beeline for the cast members manning each gate, and I see him now, moving from one gate to the next, shaking each cast member's hand, no rush, taking the time to talk, having a bit of a laugh, another handshake, and off he moves to the next gate.

I swivel back to the stage. A disturbance. Anxiety. Swan necks craning, still smiling, but worried: *Where's Josh?*

Josh is still walking the gates. He appears untroubled by the pageantry of it all and his role within it, intent, instead, on making sure that he's found all the people he needs to thank. I have no idea what's going on in his head, but it sure looks like he's viewing the event less as the formal celebration of the seventieth birthday, and more as the chance to bring thousands of cast members together—all of whom need to be looked in the eye, touched, thanked.

He looks happy, unconcerned by the increasingly frantic handlers hunting him down.

These are the ABCs in action. Josh is not bucking the corporate script: he's honoring of it, respectful of it, a stage has been prepared, and in a few minutes, he will indeed play his prescribed part. But, nonetheless, he is deliberately using this event to step into his ABCs.

We can see that he's more authentically at ease with cast members and guests than he is with the pomp and circumstance of the corporate parade. We can infer his beliefs from his willingness to duck under the ropes and go seek out the cast members hovering at the back—the ones farthest from the stage, and closest to the guests. We can begin to learn that this is a custom of his, this heading-to-the-back-of-the-room, a custom that we will now be on the lookout for at the next event, and the next. We will come to learn that this custom builds in the hearts of cast members and guests alike, until it earns its name: the Josh Effect.

Josh did not coat himself with these ABCs only once he became chairman: I have conducted day-in-the-life research with several of his predecessors and none of them acted as he does. Instead, over many years he refined his understanding of what he loved about his work; he disciplined himself to clarify and sharpen his beliefs; he turned these loves and beliefs into customs—and then all of this worked its magic to create in him a leader that thousands of cast members could rally around. And hundreds of thousands of guests could love.

You do not have the same ABCs as Josh. Your red threads are yours, not his; you may struggle with what he does effortlessly; you may value highly what he looks past; his customs might be foreign to you.

But you can do what he has done. He has taken his ABCs extraordinarily seriously. If you want people to love working for you, if you want those you serve to lean in to you, you can too. Love in the heart of someone else is kindled by the flames of your own loves—for specific activities, for deeply held beliefs, for repeatable customs. Lay this loving foundation for people, and their love for you and what you stand for will blossom.

Josh is now chatting with another gate attendant. A stage wrangler finally finds him and whispers that he has to say his goodbyes. He's needed back in the lights.

"Sorry," I overhear him saying. "I couldn't help myself."

. . .

Now, with your own ABC foundation in place, let's turn to the five feelings and what practices you can begin with your team to have them say: *Yes, I love working on this team!*

## Control: How to design experiences so your team feels in control of themselves

1. Think S.S.S.

    - S: Who do we *serve*? Ambiguity disempowers. If your team doesn't know whom they are serving, their efforts become scattered and ineffective. And if you say, "We serve everyone," this only increases their anxiety and reduces their confidence. So, be as specific as possible about the customers or stakeholders who matter most.
    - S: What *scores* (metrics) should we track? People feel in control when they can track their own progress. Avoid overwhelming them with dozens of metrics—identify the three most critical measures of success, create a dashboard of only these three, and talk about them all the time.
    - S: What *stuff* (tools, equipment) do we need? There may be no faster way to disempower your team than to be unaware that they don't have the tools they need to be productive. Get them what they need, and be seen to be listening closely to what other stuff they might need.

2. Push decision-making as close to the action as possible.

    - The best leaders empower their teams by distributing authority. When possible, let people closest to the work make the decisions, building the ownership and confidence of the ones who are closest to the front line and so have all the best and the most recent information about what's really going on. The front line is where the real intelligence lies, and so this is where most decision-making should live as well. This, in part, explains Josh's head-to-the-back-of-the-room custom.

3. Be repetitive.

    - Clarity is power. Ensure your expectations and instructions leave no room for confusion. Which means repetition. The best leaders never get bored of their own messaging. They keep saying the same things, keep espousing the same values, keep following the same customs. The only things they change are some of the stories or examples they use to bring to life whom the team serves, or what their core values are. But the specifics of whom they serve, the scores that track progress—these get repeated time and again. And the repetition empowers team members with feelings of control: they know for certain whom they're serving and how to measure their success.

### Harmony: How to create emotional alignment on your team

All team experiences are first and foremost emotional experiences. I hope you've worked on a great team, and when you did, it just *felt* different, didn't it? In your memory of this team, it's your feelings about the team that surface first. It felt exciting, and challenging, and yes, perhaps stressful, but it was somehow a good stress, the stress of the whole team being stretched to become extraordinary.

The best leaders know that feelings are the building blocks on which team excellence is constructed. The best teams operate with emotional harmony—not because everyone agrees all the time, but because they trust that their feelings are going to be surfaced and, in some practical, real-world way, honored.

1. Set a clear tone as a leader.

    - What's your default tone as a leader? Are you calm and steady? Are you passionate and energetic? Are you analytical?

A passionate guardian of the needs of the customer? There's nothing less confidence inducing that an emotionally unpredictable leader. So, present to them a consistent emotional tone, and they will be more likely to follow you around the corner.

2. Use rituals, stories, and symbols.

    - Harmony is reinforced through shared experiences. Whether it's a weekly reflection, a shared team motto, or a celebration ritual, create consistent touchpoints that reinforce connection. This is what the physical coming together of the team should be for, not for giving instructions or setting goals, because these can be done most effectively one-on-one—but instead to rally the team by showing them that, emotionally, they are all in this together.

3. Check in consistently, with light-touch frequency.

    - The best leaders don't wait for formal reviews to check in. They have weekly fifteen-minute conversations with each person, one-on-one, asking two questions: "What did you love or loathe last week?" and "What are you working on this week, and how can I help?" This simple check-in rhythm ensures that you are staying in touch with where each team member is at emotionally throughout the year. No matter how crisp and clear your goals were at the beginning of the year, events rain down upon you and your team, raising spirits one month, dampening them the next. The only antidote to constant change is constant light-touch attention. So, discipline yourself to check in with each team member for fifteen minutes each week. You don't have to act on what they share, but the sharing itself will keep you in harmony with each person.

## Significance: How to make each person feel seen on your team

Every person on your team wants to feel that their specific work matters. Their craving for significance isn't about ego; it's about contribution. Your people will stay most productive and engaged when they feel uniquely valued for what they bring.

1. Give your people a Loved it/Loathed it exercise.
    - This is a simple thing to do with each of your team: give them a blank pad, ask them to draw a line down the middle of it, write "Loved it" at the top of one column, and "Loathed it" at the top of the other, and then ask them to carry it around with them for a week. During the week, whenever they see one of the signs of a red thread, ask them to write it down in the "Loved it" column. Whenever they find themselves leaning out, procrastinating, time dragging on, write it down in the "Loathed it" column.
    - Then at the end of the week, talk through their two columns with them. Not necessarily so that you take action to change their job right away. But so that you and they can get on the same page about where they find the love in what they do. The point of this activity is awareness. On both your parts. Do it twice a year with each person and you will convey to them that you are attentive to and intrigued by where they feel at their best at work.
2. Understand their response to change.
    - Using this Loved it/Loathed it activity, try to get a read on how each person responds to change. Change is a constant in our world, and so for you to be aware of how each of your team members respond to it will give you a significant

advantage when, inevitably, change buffets the team. Some people thrive in fast-changing environments; others need stability. Some need you to present the change through a service lens, as in *This will help us serve our customers better*. Others respond to change-leads-to-innovation messaging. The closer you pay attention to how each team member reacts to change, the more you'll be able to tailor your leadership messages accordingly.

3. Individualize praise.

   - You can use the Loved it/Loathed it activity and the fifteen-minute check-in to learn how each of your team responds to praise. Obviously, each human wants to be recognized for excellent work, but such is the variation in the human condition that different people respond very differently to different kinds of praise. Some want a quiet word from you. Some want the public applause of the team. Some value money, some time off, some a letter from a happy customer. Your job is to figure which strokes work best for which folks.

## Warmth of others: How to create a sense of belonging on your team

No one wants to feel alone at work. Warmth comes from knowing that you have support, guidance, and a team that's truly there for you.

1. Offer yourself as a guide.

   - Be explicit: *I am your guide here. I know your front story, your backstory, what you're great at, what you're not, and I'm here to help you navigate work.* The data on this kind of approach is unequivocal: when team members feel they have a single point of contact at work, they are more productive, more engaged, and far less likely to leave. Explicitly offer yourself up as their single point of contact. Be their guide to help them maneuver through the often-confusing world of performance, human resources, and company policy.

2. Pair team members strategically.

    - Humans work really well in partnerships. You can certainly see this in the creative arts. Look at Taylor Swift and Jack Antonoff, Beyoncé and Jay-Z, Christopher Nolan and his wife/producing partner Emma Thomas. In business, you find Bill Gates and Steve Ballmer, Warren Buffett and Charlie Munger, Steve Jobs and Johnny Ive. Everywhere you see greatness, you see partnerships. The best leaders excel at figuring out who partners best with whom. And team members love the thought that their team leader is thinking about whom they partner best with. Not that they won't have different partners at different times, but it's confidence inducing to hear from you that you have deliberately partnered them up with someone—someone who is strong where they are less so, and who in turn can benefit from where they're strongest.

3. Define the shared identity of the team.

    - If you want your team to follow you into the future, they'll need you to tell them why you think this team will win. Tell them what the specific strengths of this team are. Show them why you think these strengths will give them a comparative advantage; why it will help them prevail. Some leaders give their team a nickname. Some rally the team around a common symbol or hero everyone identifies with. Some use adversity or the inevitable setbacks of life to give the team its identity. The methods are many, but the mandate from them to you is clear: tell them specifically what makes this team so special; then they can all step into their role on the team and add their unique specialness to the whole.

## Growth: How to create feelings of progress on your team

Obviously, people on your team will want to feel that they are moving forward. And this need is a constant. If you've never been in a leadership position before, it can come as a bit of a shock that no one ever walks into your office and announces *I'm done! I'm completely developed! You don't need to worry about me anymore! Go focus on the rest of the team!* Humans are a work in progress, and so you, their leader, have to figure out how to set up the team so that it accommodates and channels each person's craving for growth.

Fortunately, growth doesn't always mean promotions—it can mean developing new skills, gaining new experiences, and expanding one's sense of capability. They'll look to you for all of these growth opportunities.

1. Help your people learn how they learn.

    - This sounds odd, but what a powerful contribution you make to a team member when you help them learn how they learn! You would think that school or college would pay attention to this and help students figure out how they learn best. But as we all know by now, most schools and universities don't much concern themselves with the uniqueness of each student. So it falls to you to highlight how each person on your team learns. Your weekly check-ins will help greatly here. Because some on your team learn by doing, others by studying or practicing, others by copying or shadowing, and much of this detail will surface as you check in with each person week by week. Sharing what you've learned about how each person learns is an extraordinarily powerful leadership move.

2. Set micro-challenges.

    - The challenge with using yearly goals as a motivator for your team, the kind that many organizations cascade down upon each team member, and that they use to rate their performance at the end of the year, is that no one looks at these goals. Because so many of these goals are defined and stored inside human capital management software, we now know how many people go in and check their goals during the year, or alter their goals based on all the inevitable changes that occur throughout the year: 4 percent. Yes, this number may vary between teams and organizations, but the number is always vanishingly small. Corporate goals are simply invisible to most team members for most of the year, and so are virtually useless in helping your team be productive. In the face of this fact, set micro-challenges instead. Use the weekly check-in to define together a target that's a month out, put a metric to it, and then check back in in a month. Or in lieu of a performance target, define a role or an activity that the team member is going to step up and do this month—present the monthly report to the team, share one customer success story. Micro-challenges such as these create a constant tension to achieve and to grow.

3. Establish paths to mastery within roles.

    - You're lucky. Not only do humans crave learning, they also yearn for proof of learning. They love levels. And the badges and the credentials and the prestige that come with each level gained. You don't have to create this desire in your team: it's a default setting. They come with it. Your job as a leader is to channel it. And the best way to do this is to create defined levels to mastery within roles on your team. Give each level a name, define the criteria required to reach each level—it might be some combination of performance, longevity, and passing a competency test—stick to these criteria religiously (no exceptions) and then celebrate like crazy when a team member reaches a new level. The more seriously you take these levels, the more seriously they will.

. . .

To help you know how well you're doing at designing love in to the experiences of your team, I've designed a DLI X Team Metric (X stands for experience). Each item expresses only one thought. Each item contains an "extreme" word that creates a broader range of responses—a 5 is not an easy score to get. And each item asks your team member to rate only their own feelings and experiences: no item asks them to rate you as a leader, since no human is capable of reliably rating another human. (Please see my book *Nine Lies About Work* for a detailed explanation of the Idiosyncratic Rater Effect and why it renders invalid any team member's rating of the capabilities of their leader.)

Each of the five feelings is measured by two items, and then, for reliability, I've added two summary items. In aggregate, your scores on these twelve items will quantify how much love is in the system.

Obviously, you can use these items as you see fit, but for this metric to prove most useful to you, please consider the following best practices:

- Field it **four times a year**. Experiences, and the feelings they create, change frequently throughout the year. So, to keep your understanding up to date with where your team is at, I suggest using this metric once per quarter. Any more than that and they'll suffer survey fatigue. Any less, and your data will be out of date.

- For each item **pay attention only to the 5s**. As we discussed back in chapter 1, when it comes to survey data, there are 5s, which predict extreme positive behaviors, and there is everything else, which don't. So please try to discipline yourself not to take comfort in top-two-box scores. You don't field a metric such as this in order to measure team feelings. You do it to change behaviors. And only 5s predict behavior.

- A good score is a **mean of 40 percent 5s** across all items. This score will put you in the top 15 percent of all teams.

- Regardless of your current score, it's most effective to compare yourself not to some external benchmark, but instead to yourself over time. Your team will have some unique factors that might well affect how they respond to these twelve items. With these factors remaining constant, what will change is how you lead—and so, to measure this change in your leadership, pay closest attention to the **change in your own scores** from one quarter to the next.

- **Do not include new hires** (less than ninety days) in your survey. New hires are always more positive on metrics such as this. It's called the honeymoon effect: new hires instinctively rate these items more positively because they are subliminally trying to reassure themselves that they made a smart decision in joining your team. So, if you want a valid measure of how much love is in the system, wait till the honeymoon is over before you include them.

- Take action first by **examining your highest scores**. These reflect your greatest strengths as a leader, and, counterintuitively, your greatest areas of opportunity for growth as a leader. You must be doing something right in order to create these feelings in your team. So, do as the best leaders all do and take time to make sense of the experiences you're creating. What did you do to make your team feel this way? Examine this question, ask them about it, and then try to make these actions a deliberate part of your customs. Your team's scores have no inertia to them: they can come down as fast as they go up. So make sure to know what you can do to keep your highest scores high.

- When it comes time to focus on a lower-scoring item, begin with those in **control and harmony**. These are the foundations of flourishing: figure out your way of laying these foundations with your team.

- **Beware of Goodhart's Law.** This law states that as soon as a metric becomes a target, it ceases to be a metric. Which means that if you set a goal for yourself with this metric, and even tell your team about your goal, then the metric will lose its validity as a metric: people, including you, will start gaming the metric to get a certain score. Instead, think about the metric as a guide to help you identify the right actions for you to lead lovingly. Don't try to move the numbers. Do the right things for you and your team, and the numbers will move.

## THE DLI X TEAM METRIC

For each statement, rate 1–5, with 5 meaning "strongly agree" and 1 "strongly disagree."

### CONTROL

____ I know what my company truly stands for.

____ I am given everything I need to be successful in my job.

### HARMONY

____ My team loves to celebrate together.

____ Every day at work my teammates show me they care how I'm feeling.

### SIGNIFICANCE

____ At work it feels like there are people who know me extremely well.

____ I can show the very best of me at work every day.

### WARMTH OF OTHERS

____ At work my opinions always count.

____ My teammates do everything they can to help me be successful.

### GROWTH

____ At work I feel my team leader is committed to helping me learn as much as I possibly can.

____ My company shows me so many different ways to grow.

### ALL IN ALL

____ I can't imagine a world without my company.

____ My company is a force for good in the world.

Current mindSET:
**Leaders all share the same behaviors.**

DLI mindMOVE:
**The only thing all leaders share is followers.**

# 5

# Design Love In for Your Customers

There is you, the leader.

There is your team, those you lead.

And then there are your customers, those you serve.

It's time we turned our attention to them, since if you know how to design love in to your own work, and how to lead your team with love, but your customers aren't feeling it, well, you're not going to get the outcomes you want.

You can develop your experience-making skills only through real-world actions, because, when you think about it, experience-making depends on your ability to arrange, adjust, and architect the real world to make real people experience real feelings. While disciplines such as financial analysis and projection are an abstraction, experience-making is always grounded in what people actually feel.

Obviously, I can't tell you which design decisions to make in your customers' real world, but I can offer you the best way to think through, and act on, loving experience-design.

Let's start up high, at the strategy level, and then keep digging in until we arrive at the disciplines and tools you can use in any situation to design love in for those you serve.

## Love Is Strategy. Strategy Is Love

The strategy guru Michael Porter defined strategy as some combination of unique positioning, competitive advantage, and making the right trade-offs. Most of us would agree with him that figuring out the right strategy means finding the right angle of attack to generate the greatest returns on our investments.

Push a little harder on this, though, and you realize that figuring out how to get the best and longest-lasting return on your investments isn't a strategy, per se. It's a financial analysis, oftentimes based purely on various extraction tactics. It lives squarely in the amoral, transactional section of the experience continuum. And it misses the essence of strategic thinking.

Because a strategy, defined through the DLI lens, is *a sequence of experiences designed to create a set of feelings.*

Leaders who fail to understand that experience-design underpins all successful strategies fail to design successful strategies.

Remember Delta Airlines? They thought that their strategy was to maximize the return from passengers' use of their credit card. What they missed was that this was just a transactional extraction tactic; an actual strategy would have required them to create a choreographed sequence of experiences, each one carefully designed to draw passengers in so deeply they couldn't help but say *I love Delta!*

Lacking this defined sequence of experiences, the tactic, in want of a strategy, flopped.

The same will happen to United's "strategy" of monetizing passengers' personal data in their "adtech-enabled traveler media network." Lacking a designed sequence of passenger experiences, United lacks a strategy.

Another airline, Southwest, offers an even more extreme example of a leadership team mistaking investment tactics for an actual strategy.

The original strategy of Southwest, as envisioned by its colorful founder, Herb Kelleher, was a carefully curated combination of passenger experiences: the airline was to feel efficient, low-cost, short haul, all-of-us-in-this-together, flight attendants telling jokes, passengers standing in line, a captive audience as we formed our columns, A, B, and C, starting conversations as we figured out who was B16 and who was B17, a big heart on the walls of the airplanes, bags fly free, seats are up for grabs, we get on quick, have some fun in the air, and get off quick at the other end.

It was a defined and specific experience, which made some passengers fall in love with it, while others were repelled by it—just as any strategy should, and just like the strategies of Disney, Chick-fil-A, Apple, Chewy, and any organization that has been intentional about experience-design. The attraction to Southwest was impossible without the repulsion, since both were a product of the intensity and the intentionality of the experience.

Today, however, after Herb's passing, and Southwest's sale to a hedge fund, this experience is no more. Its new owners, perhaps unaware that all strategies are founded on experience-design, have ditched many of the experiences that made Southwest Southwest. The free bags are gone. The unassigned seating is gone. And so the experience of starting up conversations while standing in line is gone. And so we passengers as a captive audience for the station agent is gone. And so the jokes are gone. As is the unique Southwest-y feeling of us all in this together.

All of which could still have been strategic if the new leadership had replaced the previous precise sequence of experiences with an equally defined sequence, which, if executed excellently over time, might have become just as beloved.

But they didn't. As a frequent Southwest flyer I have received many an email from the new CEO explaining why all these changes needed to occur, and amid the typical assurances to "deliver better experiences and secure Southwest's future" there is no mention of any actual experiences at all. What will replace the unique unassigned seating experience? Nothing, apparently. What will the new Southwest do to update or renovate the quintessential Southwest warmth? Nothing. No ideas. No innovations. No mention of any real-world experiences at all.

I am writing this on a Southwest flight, as it happens. The flight attendants are still trying their very best. But as I look up and see the Southwest heart on the wall at the front of the plane, I notice it's slightly askew. Someone must have knocked it as they got up from their bulkhead seat, and no one has bothered to readjust it. What was once a proud symbol of Southwest's loving experience-design is now reduced to an obstacle, dangling on the wall.

I have no idea how big a short-term return the new owners are going to get from their removal of all the quintessential Southwest experiences. For their shareholders' sake, I hope it's significant. But this new leadership tack strikes me as strategically barren, ignoring the need to build a strategy on intentional experience-design—experiences that come to live in the hearts and minds of its customers—and so it has reduced much of Southwest to a transactional commodity, one that is now virtually indistinguishable from Spirit or Pioneer or any other low-cost airline.

Long term, they have destroyed much of the experiential value that Herb and his team took such pains to create.

Which is sad. And, from a business standpoint, wasteful.

But this is what happens when leaders fail to understand that investment decisions are not strategic decisions—they are instead extraction tactics based on projections of future transactions. Only the design of a series of experiences is strategic. Which is why experience-design is the province of all effective leaders—and why gaining skill in loving experience-design is so critical to your growth, and your success as a leader.

Of course, this is not to say that businesses don't need operational excellence. They do, and if this is all they achieve they'll locate themselves squarely in the unloving, transactional realm of the experience continuum. They will function, and, so long as they've figured out their costs and their cash flow, they will function profitably. Which is not nothing—but that's all their operational excellence will get them.

To create love in the hearts of customers, where they say *I love this! I can't imagine a world without this!* requires so much more. It requires an understanding that all effective strategies hinge on loving experience-design, and that experience-design is every single person's responsibility.

. . .

The organization that best embodies this DLI way of thinking and acting is, in my view, The Walt Disney Company. They do so many things to elevate the theme park into an intentional series of experiences—from building a thirty-foot berm around each park so that guests can't see out of the experience, to the naming of employees as cast members to reinforce the show and everyone's role within it, to leaders like Josh giving backstage tours and obsessing over trash cans—but, for our purposes now, let's look briefly at their cruise business.

Their decision to get into cruising and invest $2 billion in shipbuilding was not, in and of itself, a strategy; it was merely a bet on the financial return from all the transactions of guests booking cruises.

It became a strategy *only* when the leaders of the Disney cruise business figured out how to create a coherent and compelling sequence of experiences, which drew guests in, delighted them, led to their booking another cruise, and to telling all their friends and family to do the same. This—the design of a sequence of experiences—was the foundation of their cruise strategy.

They created retro-looking coaches to ferry the guests from the parks to the port.

They bought and developed a small private island in the Caribbean so guests could linger within the magical Disney experience even when they left the ship.

And, of course, they created dozens of live shows bringing the Disney characters and stories to life while on board.

All of this was what you'd expect from a company masterful in experience-design. But, to my mind, the most impressive example of their design intent was a rare instance where one of their design ideas did not come to pass.

I was doing a lot of work with their Imagineering group at the time, late 1996 and early 1997, and I can still remember one particular Imagineer, John Heminway, arguing passionately that the guests absolutely must be allowed to stand on the bow (the front) of the ship, and yearn, with arms outstretched, for the wide-open sea.

"This is what humans do when we set sail," he implored his fellow cast members. "If our guests are to go on their hero's journey, they will want their eyes scanning the horizon ahead!"

After raising his "This is what humans do" vision in meeting after meeting, he was eventually turned down by the highest powers that be. At the time, the conventional wisdom of cruising was that letting passengers stand on the bow of the ship was far too dangerous. Safety, the final ruling decreed, took precedence over experience.

But John's elevation of the guests' experience to the C-suite has always stuck in my mind as an exemplar of what true strategic thinking looks like. It does not look like banal financial analysis. It looks instead like passionate advocacy for the intentional creation of an experience—with the word *experience* coming up again and again, as the thing worth fighting for. The thing worth designing for. The thing without which the whole endeavor might crumble.

Disney, more than any other company I've studied, has explicitly made it every single cast member's responsibility to be an experience-maker. In the Disney world, strategy is not merely the province of the strategic-planning muckety-mucks. Strategy is experience-making, and every single cast member has a voice in experience-making.

And a responsibility always to raise their voice even if, as in John's case, their design ideas don't always come to fruition.

Postscript: In December 1997 the movie *Titanic* was released, and Jack and Rose, bodies entwined, arms reaching, manifested in every sinew John's insight about the experience we humans yearn for when we set sail.

Post-postscript: I notice that on Disney's latest cruise ships, the *Wish* and the *Treasure*, not only is the bow dramatically extended, but yes, guests are indeed now allowed to stand on it, and reach for their horizon.

Post-post-postscript: At Disney, Josh has renamed the entire resorts, parks, cruise, Imagineering, and consumer products businesses as Disney Experiences.

. . .

Rivian offers us another example of a company that weaves experience-design into all they do.

Recently the company decided to partner with Volkswagen on a $5 billion investment in proprietary EV hardware and software. But this partnership, in and of itself, isn't a strategy. It's a financial tactic to put pricing pressure on Rivian's raw material suppliers so as to extract better margins on the transaction of selling each vehicle, an operational issue that they were, and are still, working hard to solve.

In contrast, Rivian's true strategy lives squarely in the realm of figuring out how to create for their buyers a defined sequence of experiences that lead these buyers to fall in love with their Rivian.

The point of their strategy isn't to make every single person fall in love with Rivian. Instead, the point is to design such a clear, coherent, and integrated sequence of experiences that a *certain kind of person* is drawn in, one touchpoint at a time, toward the feeling of love in their heart for Rivian.

Full disclosure: I do not own, drive, or work with Rivian. And I am not for one minute suggesting that they get everything right. I am referencing them because at the time of writing they have just won *Consumer Reports*' award for the most popular car manufacturer; and, because I'm intrigued by any company that takes experiences seriously; and yes, because the data shows the two are related. A company is built one touchpoint at a time, and all other things being equal, we should always bet on the company that intentionally tries to make use of touchpoints in order to create experiences for customers. The *Consumer Reports* data suggests that this is what Rivian is currently doing quite well. It remains to be seen whether, in the coming months and years, and after government subsidies have disappeared, they continue to design love in to each touchpoint as effectively as they have thus far.

Viewed through the five feelings, here are some examples, though far from the only ones, of what Rivian is currently doing to design love in to the experiences of their customers.

## Control

Rivian gives their customers control by, among many other things, being so clear about the world these customers are entering.

It is first and foremost an adventurous world.

Their flagship vehicle is called the R1T Adventure.

Their charging network is called the Adventure Charging Network.

Their first big PR push was supplying the vehicles and batteries for Ewan McGregor's EV-powered motorcycle adventure from Tierra Del Fuego to Los Angeles, captured in the docuseries *Long Way Up*.

Not everyone wants to enter this sort of world. But that's okay. The loving thing to do is tell people very clearly what world they are about to enter, and then give them the control to decide if this world is indeed for them.

## Harmony

Rivian has vividly defined what world they want their customers to say yes to.

Harmony is the need to show your customers that you know what they're feeling, and you are meeting them right there.

Rivian does this in a multitude of ways, but the one that struck me most was their continued highlighting in their product announcements that "You can hose down the interior of your Rivian!"

What an emotionally specific way to communicate to their adventurous buyers that *Yeah, we know folks like you. We feel you. You're probably going to drag half the mountain into the truck. Don't worry. We got you. Grab a hose and spray away.*

Have you heard of any other car company encouraging you to soak your seats? No, me neither.

## Significance

Significance is our human need to feel that our unique story matters. That we are not one of many. That, when it comes to our experience, can we please have some sign that one-size-fits-one?

There's no faster way to crush this feeling than to hand us off from one anonymous touchpoint to another, and demand that we memorize and recite the details of our story to each new, disembodied voice. And so what better way to design love in to these handoffs than to give us a human who knows us, who is with us in our story, and who will advocate for us as we move through our experience.

Rivian is the only car company I know of that offers us such a human. Take a look at how she introduces herself, and imagine how loving this must feel:*

> Hi Adam,
> My name is Nicole, I'm happy to share that I'll be your Rivian Guide! I am sure you have had a lot of questions for us over

**Source:* Maria Merano, "Rivian Guides Reaching Out to R1T Reservation Holders to Prepare for July Deliveries," Teslarati, May 30, 2021, https://www.teslarati.com/rivian-guides-r1t-customer-deliveries-update/.

the previous months and I am excited to be your dedicated contact from here on out.

In the coming week, I would love to set up an introduction call with you. We'll confirm the details of your configuration and accessories and talk about your delivery timing. Feel free to click the link here to schedule our intro call.

I am available via phone, email, and SMS if you ever need to reach me, from 8:30 a.m. to 5 p.m. PT, Monday through Friday, as well as evenings and weekends for anything urgent.

Phone:

Email:

SMS:

I am looking forward to getting to know you better and supporting you on this adventure!

Stay adventurous,

## Warmth of others

As I said, I don't own a Rivian—not yet anyway.

I own a Jeep. I love my Jeep—not least because the car itself is magnificent, and the dealer I buy it from creates the five feelings at the heart of love—in his own idiosyncratic way.

But still, I'm a little disappointed. Because if ever there was a car company that should know how to offer me the warmth of others, it's Jeep.

Have you ever driven one? Then you know what I'm talking about. Every Jeep Wrangler driver is required, through some unwritten and lovely law, to wave at their fellow Wrangler drivers. Some waves are one finger cocked up from the steering hand. Some are accompanied by a sheepish grin. Some are Queenily formal. When you pass another Wrangler there is always a wave. You joined some club, and the other members are everywhere, wishing you well, nodding, waving, acknowledging your shared spirit. In our lonely and increasingly hostile world, it's a tiny beacon of solidarity, even empathy. A spontaneous and genuine sign of the warmth of others.

And Jeep, the company, does nothing with it. What a missed opportunity this is! We humans are begging for points of connection, and we feel indebted to places and people who give us this connection. Jeep ownership brings with it these connection points—and yet Jeep, the company, all but ignores them. When I bought my first Wrangler, no one told me how to play this waving game. Now, three years on, no one has tried to draw me in to it even further. Sure, there are some high-end Jeep meetups that I can sign up for on the company website. But these are expensive and, besides, they are always booked up months in advance. The pictures look great, but to me, only in a voyeuristic way. I'm never joining them in driving my Wrangler to the top of Pike's Peak.

And then there are the ducks. The rubber ducks. Someone, somewhere (apparently her name is Alison, and she's Canadian. Of course.) decided that she would start leaving a rubber duck on a fellow Wrangler's hood, along with a small note of encouragement. "It's all good." "It's probably sunny round the corner!" "You go!" Which was sweet of her. And now, oddly and delightfully, it's caught on. Jeep Ducking, it's called.

But no one's told us how to play.

My wife, Myshel, came back to our car the other day and found a pink rubber duck sitting on the door handle. *Eww. Gross!* she remembers thinking, before turning and glancing nervously around the parking lot to see which weirdo had wedged a pink duck on her door. It was only when I was writing this chapter that she suddenly realized what the duck was for. She'd mistaken a genuine sign of warmth from another human . . . as a threat. Which is a pretty good metaphor for our current social landscape. And a missed opportunity for Jeep.

Rivian hasn't missed. They have maximized many touchpoints to shape a warmth of others feeling. Their monthly newsletter shows pictures of families-like-yours, dogs-like-yours, trips-like-yours.

There's always an interview with some special Rivian owner who's just done something fun and weird with their Rivian, like faking a Rivian photoshoot to mask a marriage proposal. And, of course, there are albums of pictures of groups of Rivian drivers, just around the corner from you, doing stuff with their fellow adventurers that seems so very doable for you and your fellow adventurers.

Rivian is really working it, trying—intelligently, intentionally, and perhaps, on occasion, a little on-the-nose'edly—to bring their customers into the warmth of others. Well done them.

Jeep, come on! Yes, you need to be careful that you don't blunder into "ducking" and destroy its genuine warmth. But still, your own customers have spontaneously created warmth for others. Surely there is something loving you could do to kindle this warmth.

## Growth

This one seems obvious, but again it's interesting to compare and contrast.

I have, in the past, owned a Tesla. One of whose most gobsmacking innovations was the over-the-air software update. That my car—this hulking mass of steel and rubber—could morph into a better version of itself without any of the Sturm und Drang of dragging it to the service center was beyond belief—still is, in my view. And Tesla did, and does, a marvelous job of using this magical over-the-air Kaizen in their cars.

And yet, what a missed opportunity! Because in all my years of owning a Tesla I never got engaged by Tesla in an update or upgrade of my car. Like any human, I am delighted by the experience of having something I own get better all by itself. I would love to be involved in that experience—to be told which updates are about to happen, and where, and why, and perhaps even, for the engineery-nerds among us, how. But I never was. I never got to share in the anticipation and the thrill of excitement as my car grew a new talent. No one told me much of anything. This touchpoint was unmaximized.

In contrast, Rivian has chosen to involve their customers in the thrill of it all. By focusing on the human experience, they have changed entirely their customers' relationship to over-the-air software updates. The emails about it are frequent. The details unpacked carefully and precisely. The excitement juiced up. And hey, if you've got other things on your mind, fine—trash the email and move on with your busy life. But if you want to join in the cool experience of, and benefit from, a vertically integrated software and hardware machine called "Your Truck," then let us share with you what surprising new limb or talent your truck is about to grow.

Strategy is intentional experience-design. And Rivian is, according to their customers, currently doing it very well indeed.

. . .

To give you a sense that, as a leader, you can apply experience-design to any sort of organization, let's look briefly at one other example: Sun Bum. This is a consumer product. A sunscreen. Founded in 2010 by an entrepreneur named Tom Rinks, and sold for half a billion dollars to SC Johnson in 2019, it has since grown to be the dominant player in the sunscreen market.

Tom wasn't a follower of the humanist design principles of the likes of IDEO, Edward Deci, Don Norman, or Marc Hassenzahl; nor of the nudging, habit-forming design theories of BJ Fogg and Nir Eyal. He was just instinctively attuned to the feelings people crave, and he did everything he could think of to create these feelings in his customers.

## Control

The key control question anyone asks is: *What is this world, and how do I work it?* The world Tom wanted to invite people into was the California surfing world. Noticing that his four boys loved surfing but hated putting on sunscreen, he realized that no sunscreen company served the young, often male surf culture. So, he began by calling the company Sun Bum, the idea being that there's always a person on the beach who's hanging out, chilling, serious about their life, carefree about pretty much everything else. He's the sun bum. A beach fixture. There's something about him you can trust.

The embodiment of this feeling, this persona, became the icon of the company: Sonny, the Sun Bum gorilla.

He doesn't say anything or do anything. He's just Sonny. Tom decided to make stickers of him, and put him up everywhere surfers went—the surf shop, the local gas station, the boardwalk. By using Sonny as the icon, he was showing everyone a vivid picture of the world he was offering them. And this vividness gave them the control to choose—or choose not—to become part of this world. Sonny needed no words. He was just a gorilla. Staring at you.

*Do you want to be part of my world?* Sonny's stare asked.

## Harmony

This feeling was tricky. How could Sonny draw in these been-there-know-everything surfers, and move them to action? He couldn't berate or cajole them—they would be immediately suspicious and lean out. Surfers don't want to be sold to.

Instead, Tom needed to figure out how he could show his customers that the world they were entering knew them, knew what they were feeling, their sensibility, their lifestyle, and could meet them right there.

The best experience-makers use all sorts of different tools to achieve this feeling of harmony, such as word choice, scripts, and the five senses. Tom leveraged all of these, but, as an example, here's one of his most defining, and, in my opinion, most compelling tactics: He used a particular visual cue to signal that Sun Bum understood and felt surf culture. He looked at those pictures of endless sixties summers, and keyed in on the surfer Woodie—the car with the grained wooden side panels, and the surfboards on top. He took that textured look of the Woodie and reflected it in the sunscreen's packaging. He knew that if he did it right, he wouldn't need to explicitly hammer home that *Hey! Sun Bum gets surf culture!*—no one would believe that sort of blunt signaling. Instead, the image of the Woodie was so iconic that he knew if his sunscreen bottles replicated this image, his customers—and his boys—would instinctively make the connection themselves.

## Significance

This feeling, as you'll recall, stems from our human desire to be seen. Each of us moves through life aware that the world doesn't care about the uniqueness of our story or circumstances. Which is why we spend so much of our time armoring ourselves up against the blind will of the world. And why we find the positive self-presentation aspects of social media so enticing and rewarding.

In the case of Sun Bum, Tom wanted to give each new user of this strange, irreverent sunscreen a way to be seen as an individual. He himself had grown up feeling uncool in every way, and he brought with him into his adult life the insecurity that he was never invited to the bonfire on the beach. The cool kids were always hanging around the bonfire. Not him. He and his type weren't brought close to its warmth. They had to hang back and watch the party from the boardwalk.

Now Tom wanted to make sure that every single person would feel welcome at the Sun Bum beach bonfire. The Sun Bum beach bonfire would listen to everyone's story.

To convey the come-share-your-story-at-our-bonfire feeling—which is significance—he took a flyer. He asked his customers to take pictures of themselves doing crazy "beach things" with a Sun Bum Sonny bottle, or with a plastic Sonny, or a towel, really anything from Sun Bum. Just take it to the beach, stage it, and then send the picture to us.

He called it: "Show Us Your Bum!"

All right, not a particularly edifying name. But it was fun. It was irreverent. It was goofy. And it placed each person at the center of their own beach story.

Tom and the team were inundated with "Show Us Your Bum!" photos. Strange as it is to say, this initiative was the first and, as far as I can tell, the only time a sunscreen company has invited each customer to share their own weird and wonderful beach story.

The customers loved it. And they moved one step closer to falling in love with Sun Bum.

## Warmth of others

The other day I asked Tom what he and his team did to create a feeling of community around his product. I think I was struggling with how a consumer product could genuinely bring into a customer's life the warmth of other humans.

Sure, I understood how an entertainment/hospitality company such as Disney might be able to draw guests together into a shared experience. And I could see how lifestyle products such as a person's car could be leveraged to show the kind of community the person was joining.

But a consumer product? How, I wondered?

This is the text he sent back. In a second. I've never gotten a quicker reply:

> In retail you have mass, pharmacy, club, grocery, and small independent mom-and-pop small boutique shops—or surf shops in Sun Bum's case, which are called "specialty." These small retailers exist for the people who want something that isn't available at Walmart or a Target or grocery store chain. They want to be unique.
>
> When Sun Bum launched in 2010 these "specialty" shops were selling the same sunscreens (Coppertone, Banana Boat,

> Hawaiian Tropic) that you could find at CVS and the gas station across the street.
>
> We offered them something "special" that could only be bought at their store, and without having to compete on price with mass retail chains.
>
> These little family-owned shops were the lifeblood of our community, and a lot of them were struggling to make it with all the big chains that were moving in that could buy in bigger volumes and sell at cheaper margins. We made something (Sun Bum) just for them. To help them be different. To help them compete and fight to survive another season. These shops were our favorite shops in towns run by our favorite people and families and friends. We loved helping drive traffic to their businesses.

So, yeah, there are always ways to bring a community together—in this case, the specialty mom-and-pop boutiques—and show them that they're not alone.

## Growth

The last loving feeling is growth. The sense that whoever or whatever is delivering this experience is aware that time moves on, and that tomorrow you will have to wake up and face the day feeling—hopefully—just a little more capable than you were yesterday.

As with the other feelings, there are many tools a leader can use to create the feeling of *This experience made me bigger!* Tools such as teaching you a new skill, or offering you a new perspective or resource. One of the best tools, though, is inspiration. If the experience can raise your sights and help you see that you are a part of something bigger than yourself, you'll lean in to it. You'll want to be a part of it. You'll love it.

Here's Sun Bum's elegant way of lifting your sights. They didn't need a mission statement. Nor a public commitment to their "Why."

They just needed a way to show every single Sun Bum customer, and every single beachgoer, and every bonfire partier, every son, every daughter, every mom and dad, what they were all a part of.

They took out ads in magazines, created mammoth billboards, and designed aerial banners to fly over beaches, all proclaiming the same thing: "We don't care if you use ours. Just use sunscreen."

The bigger point of Sun Bum was not just to sell more Sun Bum. It was to persuade customers, beginning with Tom's four boys, that if you're going to hang out at the beach, you'd better use sunscreen.

You might say, *Well, doesn't every sunscreen company say this?* No, apparently, they don't. Only Sun Bum thought it important enough to tell their customers that Sun Bum wasn't the point. That staying safe in the sun was the point.

You might say, *Well, designing a billboard isn't a particularly grand gesture. It's just a billboard.* And you'd be right. Lifting the sights of his customers and, in this case, finding a genuine, non-corporate-sounding way of showing them how Sun Bum thinks about them and their tomorrows wasn't a complex or expensive undertaking.

But it was a design decision. It was an intentional shaping of a feeling, in order to shape a behavior, and thence an outcome.

Tom is no academic. He's just like you: a leader of a business trying to figure out how to get people to fall in love with his product. Who comes up with Sonny? Who thinks about making a sunscreen tube that evokes a Woodie? Who tells their customers to "Show us your bum"? Yes, it takes a certain kind of mind to put all that together, and create, from whole cloth, a product, a brand, and most importantly a series of experiences that upends a multibillion-dollar market.

And yet you—and the people you lead—have within you this kind of design thinking. You have this power.

You can apply the five feelings to your own situation. You can use them as a blueprint for asking yourself what you can do in the real world to foster those five feelings in those you serve. Use those five feelings as a spur for your creativity. Use them to become passionate about, and effective at, experience-design. Use them to create your strategy.

# 6

# The Three Disciplines to Design Love In

"Where do I start?" Mikey asks. "I've got over two hundred people in the company. How do I reach them all? What do I tell them to go do?!"

Mikey's an entrepreneur. An excellent one. Together with his two uncles he's opened seven restaurants and bars in Southern California, all very carefully designed to convey a distinctive promise and atmosphere to the customers. Lumi is a sushi place: perched on a rooftop accessible only through a secret elevator, it gives off a futuristic Tokyo *Kill Bill* sort of vibe. Huntress is a modern high-end steak experience, all swooping chandeliers and Carrara marble bar tops. Rustic Root is a beach-adjacent brunch sort of place, which somehow, in its decor, manages to be both casual and elegant.

Walk into any one of Mikey's restaurants and you instinctively know that you're in a place where someone has taken the word *experience* seriously—at least they have in terms of the physical design of the restaurant, and of the menu of items they serve.

What Mikey's after is what every leader is after: an actual experience that is as defined and as intentional as the look of the Lumi elevator or the color of Huntress banquettes (light green.) And it's here he starts to feel a little less sure of himself. He knows how to construct a pristine, hyper-functional and efficient kitchen, but not necessarily how to create an experience in that kitchen that creates love in the hearts of the chef, sous-chefs, and food runners. He's creative enough to design and build an ice-cream-sundae-at-your-table cart, and to train servers in how to make the sundae tableside—but he becomes less precise in knowing how to teach each server what to say to turn the sundae cart into a loving experience.

Simply put, his real-world challenge is: How do I build this "design love in" muscle across my entire company? Where do I start, and where does it go from there?

Or in Mikey's words: "Give me a break! I'm not Disney! It's just me and my uncles here, trying to make memorable experiences for our guests!"

So, if you are a Mikey, or if you know a Mikey, or if you work for a Mikey, and you are not a Disney with their hundred-year heritage of experience-making, what teamwide or companywide disciplines can you start to design experiences people love?

Here are three disciplines you can start tomorrow: these disciplines prompt you to examine an experience to see what you're currently doing, and guide you to how and where you can do it more lovingly.

1. Walk the Stage
2. Equip the People
3. Sequence the Scenes

To bring each to life, I'm going to ask you to zoom out from Mikey's world, and instead take in the whole of Kroger.

Kroger doesn't have seven locations. They have more than twenty-seven hundred.

Founded in Cincinnati back in 1883 as the Kroger Grocery and Baking Company by an enterprising young man named Barney Kroger, the modern-day Kroger is massive. At these twenty-seven hundred stores work more than four hundred thousand associates, serving close to twenty-two million customers a day. Under the Kroger umbrella now live a whole host of different banners acquired through acquisition, such as, in the West, Ralphs, Smiths, and King Soupers, and in the Midwest, Dillons.

They have always been the leading innovator in their sector. Kroger was the first to bring baked goods and meat into the same store as hard goods, the first to let customers self-select, the first to do home delivery—via horse-drawn wagon—the first to accept telephone orders—in 1905!—the first to do food quality control, first to put expiration dates on products, first to scan items using bar codes—and have long been lauded for their ability to stay agile and flex their operations to fit the changing expectations of their customers. In fact, in *Good to Great* Jim Collins juxtaposed Kroger with A&P, with the latter refusing to accept the need for supermarkets, while the former recognized the customers' desire for convenience and committed to a decades-long investment in creating huge "marketplaces" where customers could find everything from milk to organic produce to clothing to prescriptions, and so make meal times simpler.

Despite this nearly hundred-and-fifty-year heritage, and the plaudits of business experts, Kroger projects a never-satisfied feeling. At least it does to me. A little while back I met a chap by the name of Tim Massa. By title Tim is the Executive Vice President and Chief Associate Experience Officer of Kroger, but in person he comes across as something more. He's the leader who holds it all together, who, when Kroger went through some challenging times with a stalled merger with Albertsons and leadership changes at the very top, is the person everyone at all levels relies on to keep the ship steady and the eyes facing forward. He's clearly got some measure of position power, but you sense that he wields more than purely his position alone would suggest. His is a quiet power. Born, in my experience of him, from a core belief in the goodness of people, and a willingness to be there for his people, no matter how trying the circumstances.

Tim's question to me was this:

> At Kroger our commitment is to "feed the human spirit." We have a heart on the wall in all our break rooms to symbolize that we don't just sell food for your table—we truly care about everyone in our communities. And yet, we don't fully operationalize this heart. We feel it. We have publicly committed to it. But we want to do more. What more can we do to operationalize love, at scale, across two thousand seven hundred stores, hundreds of thousands of people, and twenty-two million customers?

Here's what they did. Well, more accurately, here's what they started—this work is not finished and if they get it right, it never will be. It will become an organizational competency, something they get better and better at, and because it'll be designed in so deeply, so woven into the fabric of the company, it'll be impossible to copy. It will create love in the hearts of associates and customers through an embedded mastery. If Kroger succeeds in sticking to these disciplines, then fifty years from now their business will be flourishing precisely because they have created loving feelings in the hearts of associates and customers. They will have become, at scale, *masters* of loving experience-design. And they will have done this little by little, one leader, one team, one touchpoint at a time.

As will you, with your team, your customers, your touchpoints.

## Kroger: Operationalizing "Like to Love"

First off, they started small. In Kroger's case this meant sixteen stores in and around Cincinnati, close to the home office so this group of stores could be most easily "geared" to others, and the learnings spread more efficiently to other divisions, other stores.

Second, the company chose a leader who everyone knew believed passionately in creating loving experiences for Kroger associates and customers. Ten years ago, Ann Reed, a thirty-year Kroger veteran and the president of the Cincinnati/Dayton division, had launched an initiative she called "Like to Love"—she didn't have the data to reinforce her belief that she could actually elevate the store experience from "Like to Love," nor what measurable outcomes would be driven if she did, but her instincts anchored her belief nonetheless. Ann had been walking down this road for a decade, and so she was the obvious choice to lead a more intentional initiative. People knew she carried it close to her heart. It was Ann just being Ann.

Of course, the lesson for you here is, don't try to design love in if you don't believe it. As we discussed in reference to AI, and to Josh at Disney, love's power lies in its authenticity, and specifically, the authenticity of its intention. Since love is the *deep and unwavering commitment to the flourishing of a human*, the human's flourishing is the moral starting point and ending purpose for everything. If you don't believe this, or if your leader doesn't believe this, then please don't try to manufacture the DLI techniques. People will sniff out that your intentions aren't authentic, aren't focused on the flourishing of the human, and so their guard will go up.

And if ever you're struggling to get in touch with what your true intentions are—which can be tricky, as you make your way through our loudly transactional world—simply return to those foundational questions from chapter 1:

> "Do you want your customers to love your company?"
>
> "Do you want your people to love working here?"

If you can genuinely answer yes, then keep going. If no, for whatever reason, then fine—but I'd recommend not trying the techniques of loving experience-design. They'll likely produce the exact opposite outcomes of what you want.

As I'm writing this, Starbucks has just announced that they're getting back to their roots, part of which is telling their baristas to start writing the names of the customers on the cups, and, in addition, writing something uplifting on the cup. This is a good tactic, in theory. The challenge, of course, is that if you make it a mandate—which they have done—then all of a sudden, we slide toward the unloving end of the experience continuum: Does this barista genuinely wish me well? Or are they writing their little uplift phrase because they will get punished if they don't? Is it real? Or is it merely transactional?

If we customers suspect it's the latter, this tactic immediately registers as inauthentic. Up go our barriers, and we start to lean out. When you mandate love into a touchpoint, you get from us the opposite of love. You get suspicion and all the negative behaviors that come with it.

Kroger was sensitive to this. And so, after carefully selecting a leader whose authenticity was unimpeachable, they then turned their attention to the three disciplines.

This is what operationalizing love looked like in the Kroger-land of Northern Kentucky.

## Discipline 1: Walk the Stage

To design love in to an experience, you first have to walk the stage of that experience. Walk it with an eye not to your company's own systems or processes, but instead through the lens of the people actually having an experience—which in this case means the customers and the associates.

You can do this. I'm not saying it's easy: walking the stage requires you to set aside your assumptions and your expertise, your jargon and your jadedness, and just let your senses lead you around the stage.

But you can do this.

I say this because Joey could. Joey has been working for Kroger for even longer than Ann. He's now a district operations lead, which means he's the one every store leader turns to for all the standard operating procedures and functional process requirements for the efficient running of the stores. He would never call himself this, but he's the operations police. The final word when people want to double-check what's allowed.

And yet he was able to walk through aisles he could've navigated blindfolded, and see vividly what was really on the stage. The stage as it was. Not the stage as he wished it would be.

And what he saw right away was what I imagine you will see when you walk your stage. He saw visual noise. Signs in customers' line of sight, but signs that were actually intended for associates. Signs that one department had created clashing with signs another department had created, leaving the customer to try to figure out which sign meant what to whom. He saw signs with jargon on them that made sense to Kroger, but that no customer would ever understand.

He was following a research protocol called Natural Experience Processing: basically, he set aside his grooved route through the store, and instead followed wherever one of his five senses took him. If the smell of the bakery drew him toward it, he let himself be drawn. If he felt himself confused by where to stand at the deli counter during the lunch rush, he let himself feel it, and then allowed himself to do what those confused feelings nudged him to do: which in this case meant "walk away from the deli counter."

If he saw a sign saying "Fresh for Everyone" in front of a display of Halloween cobwebs, he registered the incongruity, and steered clear of it—as any customer would.

And as Joey, and a team of other leaders, walked the stage as it is, they started to take note of what needed to be cleared off the stage. Walking the stage led to clearing the stage.

When you walk your stage, you'll find yourself doing this as well. With your senses alert, and your mind and heart open, you'll find yourself bumping into items on the stage that don't need to be there; in Joey's case, he was literally bumping into some of these items; in your case, an item on the stage might be an email, or a slide deck, or a meeting, or a customer service script.

But like Joey, you'll walk the stage and start realizing that there's a lot of clutter on the stage. Some of this clutter was left over from a previous "play" that no one had bothered to remove. Some of it was the by-product of two "playwrights" fighting over whose play is actually being performed—different departments, with different priorities. Some of it was a function of many playwrights being unaware that all plays have to play out on the same stage, in front of customers.

However the clutter came to be on there, walking the stage will inevitably lead to you clearing the stage of these holdover items. Please discipline yourself to remove these items before you attempt to do anything else. You can build love in the hearts of your customers only if they understand what you're trying to say to them, or do for them, or move them through, and all of this intention will be lost in the noise—until you remove the noise.

So, job one for you, as it was for Joey and his team: walk the stage and clear the stage. Say less, before you gear up to say more. Designing love in means first designing noise out.

And as you're walking the stage, you'll begin to start seeing the outline of the story you want to tell your customers. This is important because for the audience to fall in love with their experience, they need to hear your story. This story shows them what you stand for, and what mark you want to leave on the world. Remember, the first feeling of love is control, and one way to give people control is to tell them very clearly who you are for them. What world you are asking them to step into.

If you're Disney or Rivian or Sun Bum, you know from the get-go what story you're asking people to step into. The story work for these companies is done, and now everyone in the company simply has to find their way to tell their part of the story.

But in most companies, the story work is *not* done. The story is *not* clearly defined. It's there somewhere. But it's opaque. Your team and your customers struggle to tell it to themselves or to others.

So, to find yours, use your stage-walking as the real-world way to start defining your story. Use your assessment of *What are we currently having people experience?* to answer for yourself:

> "What story are we currently telling?" and
>
> "Is this the story we want to be telling?"

At Kroger the initial answer to the first question was that the company wasn't entirely sure what story the real-world experience was telling. There were a great many touchpoints—carts in the parking lot corrals; "Get Your Free Vaccine" signs at every turn; bright, shiny fresh produce, perfectly displayed in Rothko-esque color bands; heavily marked-down "Last Chance" items that were less than perfectly displayed; brand-name signage in almost all departments, some of which Kroger owned—Blumhaus flowers, Murray's cheese—and some of which they didn't—Snowfox sushi, Boar's Head deli meats.

It was a lot to take in and make sense of, even for a forty-year veteran like Joey.

But as they kept walking the stage, certain patterns of experiences—real-world experiences, not slogans or taglines—began to emerge.

At the bakery department they bump into a team lead who proudly shows them the six-foot-tall cupcake display she's made, explaining excitedly why she'd chosen the frosting for each part of the display, and what she loved most about designing cakes.

In the produce department, an associate is seen explaining to a customer how making a lettuce squeak is the best way to judge its freshness.

At the cheese shop, a certified Murray's cheesemonger comes out from behind the counter not just because she wants to explain why this particular "boozy blue cheese" is her favorite, and why "blue cheese isn't blue, it's just misunderstood," but also to roll up her sleeve to reveal the blue cheese tattoo on her forearm.

At the deli counter, the associate leans over to describe in detail how he comes to learn not just which meats each regular customer prefers, but also the precise width of the slicing, and why satisfying the "uber-thin slicers" is the most fun and trickiest part of his job.

These associates aren't just being friendly, or trying to impress in that one moment. They are clearly into their craft, and they have been for a good long while. They are artisans, proud of their expertise, proud to share it in displays, tips, techniques, and tattoos.

Another pattern, hiding in plain sight, is each Kroger store's connection to its local community. Joey and team hear customers talk about "My Kroger," referring to the specific neighborhood store they consider their own. They see "local" signage displays featuring various products from the surrounding farms. They walk into the lobby of the store in Independence, Kentucky, and are met with hundreds of framed, mostly black-and-white photographs of men and women in service. It turns out these are the relatives of regular customers of this Kroger store: customers are invited to bring in a photograph of a relative in the military, the Kroger team frames it, and then a small ceremony is held in the store as the picture is added to the wall of local heroes.

These patterns start to coalesce into a story about who Kroger is in the world. It's a story about food quality and food expertise, about artisans passionate about their craft, and about the local customers they serve.

This is what you'll find when you walk your stage. From all the many touchpoints you encounter, certain patterns will emerge, patterns that have the potential to come together into a clear story about who you are for people.

But stories don't tell themselves. So, once you begin to discern a pattern, your job will be to define the details of your story. And for your story to resonate most deeply with your audience it will need to have certain characteristics. It will need to be *authentic*—your audience is far more likely to believe a story that they instinctively feel is true. It will need to be *simple*—for the story to live on in your audience's mind and heart, it needs to be one that they can retell, to themselves and others. And it will need to be *unique*—it needs to be a story that only you can tell.

As Kroger sought to define their story, they looked back to their past, to who they had always been for people, as you will, if you are to define a story that is authentic, simple, and unique to you.

And in their past they began to find examples of certain patterns stretching back more than a century and a half. Local patterns: contrary to the practice of some of their competitors, they'd instinctively chosen to keep the banners of the companies they'd acquired because local communities love "their Ralphs," "their Fred Meyer," "their Frys." Their founder, Barney Kroger, was a dedicated investor in his local Cincinnati community: he was the president of the Cincinnati Welfare Association for the Blind, founded the Kroger Hills Camp to combat anemia in children, and even donated the first five tigers to the famous Cincinnati Zoo.

If Kroger wanted to define part of their story around "local," it would have the benefit of being true.

They also found in their past a century-and-a-half-long dedication to food quality and expertise.

Barney Kroger's earliest quotes, found in newspaper article microfiches, all related to his promise of food quality.

"Be particular. Never put anything on our shelves we wouldn't put on our own tables."

"Beware of basement bread!" (The bread that some bakers used to "find" in the basement when all other stocks had been depleted.)

It was this passion for food quality that led to his creation of the first Product Quality Lab in the 1920s, and, after his passing, to the first sell-by dates on products in the 1970s. And more recently, to Kroger investing in the expertise of their mongers by sending the best Murray's cheese associates to the weeklong Murray's certification course in New York.

If Kroger wanted to highlight the quality and expertise part of their story, it would, again, have the benefit of being true.

And if they combined these two patterns—"dedication to local" and "committed to artisans"—they would also be able to tell a story that was unique, a story only Kroger could tell.

The way I'm describing this, you might be thinking: *Well, of course that's the story Kroger should be telling associates and customers! It's right there in their past and their present!*

But what Kroger found, and what you may well find, is that you can get so close to your own story that you can't hear it anymore. Or, you hear it so often you get bored of it, and start trying to tell a cacophony of new and different stories.

The truth about love—and the key to designing it in to experiences—is that clarity is loving. Associates and customers don't want you to keep telling new stories: they might interest you, but they are unloving to those you lead and serve. To be loving is to be clear about the world you are asking others to enter. This clarity gives them the control to choose—to enter it, or not—and this feeling of control is, as you now know, the first step toward love in their heart for you and your company.

Remember, the opposite of design is drift; over time you get too close to your story, too familiar with it, and as you lose its thread, it frays and unravels, drifting further and further away into nothingness until you, the leader, and they, your customers, can't remember it anymore. This discipline of walking the stage anchors you back into the reality of what story you are currently telling, and what story you truly want to tell.

This discipline, when done intentionally, stops drift.

## Discipline 2: Equip the People

In most, if not all, organizations, the people bring your story to life.

As your story is coming into sharper focus, you will start to look at the specific people who can carry this story and the props they will use to tell it. Of course, in a sense, every single person is a touchpoint in the experience you're making, as is every prop. And yet, if you examine closely the story you're wanting to tell, you'll discover that certain people are more central than others to your story.

In Kroger's case they realized that if they were to tell an "expertise lives here" story, then in each department the artisans themselves would become stars of the show. And so, in practical terms, they started asking themselves: What do we need to do to be more intentional about showcasing our experts?

> *The Murray's certified cheesemongers get to wear a special red jacket—should we design special uniforms for experts in other departments?*
>
> *Should we create precise certification requirements for expertise in each department, and put up signage that highlights which certification level each associate has reached?*
>
> *Should we change the height of the counters, or their layout to make it easier for customers to meet and speak with these artisans?*
>
> *Should we hang nicely framed photographs of our artisans so that customers can recognize them and come to seek them out?*
>
> *Should we include customer invites for special events in our artisans' lives, such as when a certified monger gets to cut her first Parmesan wheel?*

And in terms of props:

> *Currently we ask various departments to sample their products once a week. Should we make sampling a more frequent and predictable part of the Kroger shopping experience?*
>
> *Should we more precisely script our artisans so that they know the point of sampling is less to sell product, and more to channel their expertise, and to deepen our relationships with customers through a shared love of the product?*

*Should we organize learn-at-Kroger events where our artisans showcase their craftsmanship by teaching our customers the secrets of preparing fresh fish, or how to maintain their flowers to prolong their life and beauty?*

*Should we leverage some of our company-owned brands, such as Private Selection, to make a line of recipes created and curated by our named artisans—recipes that are beautifully designed and on display in each department?*

They found, as you will, that once you've defined key elements of your story, the role of certain people and the possibilities of certain props become compelling. Almost to the point that you can't *not* activate some of these ideas because they are so obviously in service of the story you are trying to tell.

As of this writing I don't know which of these activations Kroger has enacted. I do know that disciplines 1 and 2 combined to unleash the company's creativity. And as with you, so long as Kroger sticks to these disciplines, it will be able to bring to life through its people an explicitly designed experience, one based on a story only Kroger can tell.

## Discipline 3: Sequence the Scenes

The third discipline asks you to think about the sequence of the experience.

In the broadest sense, every experience has a before, a during, and an after, but, more precisely, each experience—whether it's a making-a-reservation experience, or a product fulfillment experience, or an insurance claim-processing experience—can be broken down intentionally into a sequence of scenes. And then each scene can be designed to achieve a certain set of feelings, using specific "songs" designed in to each scene.

For Kroger the sequence of some scenes of the customer shopping experience was obvious. First comes the parking lot scene. Then the entryway scene, with the corral of carts and the hand-sanitizer wipes. Then the produce department scene, drawing the customer into the store with its color-banded displays of freshness. A lot of good work could be, and has been, done in each scene to design love in.

In other experiences the sequence was less apparent. For example, when you enter the deli department, do you take a number first and then start to survey the products' display? Or do you survey first, and then talk to fellow customers to figure out who's next, in a Southwest-boarding-area kind of way?

When your Kroger visit involves buying balloons, are you supposed to buy them first and then leave them with the floral associate while you go about the rest of your shopping? Or do you complete your entire shop first, and then stop at the floral department at the end right before you go through the cashier line?

You might think these sequencing considerations are trivial, but to a customer they all matter. Think about those first three feelings of love: control, harmony, and significance. Let's say you've gone to your Kroger to pick up some balloons for your daughter's high school graduation, and you're in a bit of a rush because you forgot to get them last night, the graduation's today, the party's this evening, and you still have to buy all the beverages and the cupcakes. How can proper sequencing of your experience create—or crush—these first three feelings of love? (This is a nontrivial example for Kroger since, among other considerations, they are the largest florist in the world, and this part of their business generates upwards of $1 billion a year in revenue. They've got to get this experience right!)

Looking at this scenario two different ways: In a store lacking an intentional sequence, you, the customer, run to the store at 7 a.m., hoping to grab your balloons before the rush of other customers. Because it's so early, no one's there to help you. So, you decide to go get all the other items you need, returning to the floral department only once your cart is full. But by this time, a crush of other customers has descended on the floral department and now it's a thirty-minute wait for your darn balloons. So, you ditch the balloon buying, pay for your other items, and head home. You'll buy your balloons elsewhere.

Or, flipping the sequence around: You go early to the store, and as before you find no one there to help. But you're pushy, so you grab someone from another department, and they go in the back to find and blow up your balloons. So far so good. They then wander off, back to their real department where they have other work to get done, leaving you with a dozen helium balloons floating above your cart. What are you supposed to do with them? You can't leave them in floral, unattended. You can't drag them around the rest of the store while you shop for all your other items.

And so, stuck in an undesigned sequence, you opt for buying only your balloons and decide to get all your remaining items from a different store closer to your home.

In both scenarios Kroger not only loses your revenue, they also lose the opportunity to create love in your heart. In each scenario you feel disempowered by your confusion about who's there to help you—so no control. You feel no sense that anyone cares why you're buying balloons, or what you might be feeling as you dash in—so no harmony. And nothing in the experience has given you the feeling that anyone in the store has the time or the attention to find out what your front story for coming to the store might be today, who the balloons are for, and what the occasion is—so no significance.

You're just a rushed, lonely, disoriented customer, who will never tell anyone about your experience buying ballons at Kroger for your daughter's graduation. It will be an instantly forgettable experience for you and a missed opportunity for Kroger.

And all because no one had thought through the best sequence for your experience, and then designed scenes and "songs" especially for this sequence.

This kind of design work is precisely what the Kroger team began to address. In the case of the balloons their loving-experience-design thinking looked like this:

> Yes, we know that customers can order balloons online, but we also know that many customers arrive early at our stores to buy balloons. So, the first part of the sequence is defined by a customer running in—perhaps slightly anxious to get the right color balloons, perhaps feeling rushed, perhaps also happy to be celebrating a particular family event.
>
> We actually want the customer to buy the balloons *first*, rather than complete the rest of their shop and then return to floral. Because by this time there might indeed be a longer line of customers, and they might decide to ditch the balloon buying with us.
>
> So, instead, we will design an experience to encourage the customer to complete their balloon buying *first*.
>
> We will staff accordingly so that an associate is there and ready to step into their role in the scene.
>
> Then to help them play this role, we will design a "song" for each floral associate in which we encourage them to ask the customer what the occasion for the balloons is, and, depending on the answer, to suggest other items that might match the occasion—cupcakes and streamers for a graduation, cards and wrapping paper for a birthday.
>
> As part of this "song" this associate will ask the customer if they would like to leave the balloons in the floral department so they can do the rest of their shopping unburdened by a dozen purple balloons bouncing off aisles and endcaps.

Take a minute to imagine how this customer would feel. They are immediately empowered by the presence of the associate waiting there for them—an associate who has clearly thought through what else they might want to get done in the store, and is ready with practical advice to help them navigate their various shopping needs (control).

This associate recognizes what they might be feeling—stress to get the balloon buying done, anxiety about what to do with a flock of balloons in the narrow aisles (harmony.) And gives them a practical plan for how to alleviate these feelings.

And yes, the associate bothers to learn just a little about what they might be celebrating, and so they feel seen (significance). They're not just another transaction to get through; they're a parent celebrating a significant family milestone. And Kroger now gets to be a small part of that.

The customer might also feel the warmth of others, as this associate steps into the middle of their urgency and anxiety and offers themselves up as a guide—a person who's got their back as they try to juggle all their responsibilities that morning.

And of course, the upshot of these feelings is that the customer behaves differently. Amid the frenetic, checklist nature of their day, this one experience drew them in, so much so that they stay longer in the store, perusing the aisles, confident that, back in floral, their balloons—and the celebration they're responsible for—are in safe hands.

Later in the day they remark to a friend how easy it was. Later that month, when they need a big bouquet for a friend's birthday, they don't think twice: of course they're going back to their Kroger. And when they do, because the experience has been deliberately designed for love, they have the same kind of experience, and so they feel the same feelings once again.

The customer doesn't see all the sequencing, or all the intentional design work. They just feel the feelings—and little by little, one visit after another, one interaction after another, they lean in, and love grows in their heart.

This is a simple—and real—example of how being intentional about an experience's sequence leads to a series of practical decisions about how each scene in the sequence can best be designed, and which "songs" can add most to the experience. This is what intelligent experience-making looks like in the real world. It is not complex. Nor expensive. Nor abstract. It's just a series of practical decisions, triggered by selecting intentionally the sequence, scenes, and songs of an experience.

You yourself can do this with any of your experiences. As you do—using the five feelings as your guide for what each scene of the sequence is trying to achieve—you'll build your mastery at experience-making. And those you serve will feel differently, and so will behave differently.

. . .

Remember that the foundation of what you're doing is quite simple: you are putting yourself in the shoes of a person going through an experience. All the way through an experience. You are imagining a human moving from one touchpoint to the next, and thinking about what this human would want from each touchpoint. What would calm them down. What would lift them up. What would cause them to lean one step further into the experience. What would cause them to say, "I loved that!"

Yes, this is hard to excel at, but it is easy to begin. Just think about this person, and then move with them through time. Discipline yourself to do this for all the experiences you're making, and quite soon it will become habitual. All sorts of practical activations will reveal themselves to you. You'll act on some of them, learn from the reaction, adjust them, and then act on them again. And gradually you'll build up your experience-making muscle so that it becomes stronger, more flexible, something you instinctively rely on to elevate your team's performance—where you are intentionally creating love in the hearts of those you serve.

Since measurement improves performance, I've designed for you a DLI X Customer Metric. Please use it to keep track of how much love-in-the-system you've created, and in which direction you're trending. Let these twelve simple statements help you and your team track your success as experience-makers.

And as before, the same best practices apply to this metric as to the DLI X Team Metric.

- Field it **once per quarter** so your customer data stays fresh.
- Getting **40 percent 5s** puts you in the top 15 percent of our database.
- Ideally, you will compare **yourself to yourself** over time.
- Focus first on those items where you have the **highest scores**, so you can design in practices and actions to keep those high scores high.
- When you turn your attention to your lower-scoring items, focus first on the **control and harmony** items.
- Beware of **Goodhart's Law**. Don't use the metric as a target to hit, but instead as a spur to keep experience-making front and center for you and your team. Do this intentionally and intelligently, and your numbers will move.

## THE DLI X CUSTOMER METRIC

For each statement, rate 1–5, with 5 meaning "strongly agree" and 1 "strongly disagree."

**CONTROL**

____ My experience felt extremely well-organized.

____ I love what this company stands for.

**HARMONY**

____ I love how my experience made me feel.

____ My experience was perfect for people like me.

**SIGNIFICANCE**

____ This company is genuinely interested in me.

____ When I needed personal attention, they took all the time I needed to help me.

**WARMTH OF OTHERS**

____ I know exactly whom to call for help at the company.

____ This company has my back.

**GROWTH**

____ This company has taught me something really useful.

____ The company is always showing me how to be a smarter customer.

**ALL IN ALL**

____ I can't imagine a world without this company.

____ I will definitely recommend this company to friends and family.

# 7

# Your Road to DLI Mastery

Up till now, we've covered:

- The *one* lens you can use to split the world into loving and unloving, and so call things by their real name. Such is the beginning of wisdom, and wise action.
- The *two* roles that you, the DLI leader, can learn to play, Mover and Maker.
- The *three* disciplines that can focus your efforts to design love in to the experiences of team members and customers.

Each of these, in combination, forms an excellent foundation on which to build your DLI skill.

If you would like more, if you would like to take the next steps toward real mastery in this skill, in this chapter I offer you further levels of DLI application: specifically, *four* tools and *five* accelerators.

## The Four Tools to Loving Experience-Design

While you may discover your own distinct approach, from all the research I've conducted it does appear that the best experience-designers use four distinct tools. Learn how to apply these tools to the experiences of those you lead, and those you serve, and you will go a long way toward creating love in their hearts and all the goodness that comes with it.

## 1. BDA: Look at the before, the during, and the after

Every experience has a before, a during, and an after.

When I went to that Coldplay concert, my experience didn't begin when the band jumped on stage. Instead it began when I saw—on social media, as it happens—that their tour was coming to my city, and I started to poke around online to find the best dates and tickets. While I didn't think the band had a hand in my experience of ticket buying, it became part of the way I felt about the whole experience, just as the "battle of the parking lot" did.

Before you go to the grocery store you have a vivid and detailed experience of the grocery store. And not just in their ads or social media postings. You have their bags lying around your house. Their receipts live on your countertops. Their name-brand food items sit in your fridge. Each of these items lives in your awareness, and drip by drip, adds to your flow of thoughts and feelings about the grocery store—*before* you've set foot in it.

The during part of an experience is more obvious and gets the most attention. From Coldplay's documentary *A Head Full of Dreams* I know that Chris and the band spent countless hours parsing every aspect of the concert experience, from the major—which songs will make the set list—to the minor—what color should the bracelets be during their hit single "Yellow." (Yep, yellow.)

And then there's the after—which, frankly, gets far less of the attention. And yet, as I discovered, and Daniel Kahneman and Barbara Fredrickson have documented, the final feelings you're left with often turn out to be the most powerful in terms of defining your long-standing feelings of the experience.

Why did the best doctors think so carefully about helping each patient "know what to do at home to alleviate their condition"?

Because they had deliberately thought about the patient's life after their experience with the doctor was over.

Audi lost sight of the after of my experience coming to the end of my lease, and as a result lost me as a customer for the next five years.

Why did Disney create the role of the VP of Parking—the person whose entire job is to ensure not only that the processes and layout of the parking are working efficiently, but who also creates systems to ensure that they can keep track of which cars might have left their lights on and are ready with battery chargers when the guests return to their car? Because they know that guests make sense of their day at the park as a holistic experience, one that includes the leaving.

And as you now know, I would never tell you to go to a Coldplay concert because of what happened as we were fighting our way home.

So, to start mastering your skill at experience-design, draw yourself a graph like the one in figure 7-1, and then write down what you imagine the person you're serving, or leading, is experiencing before, during, and after their experience. What is happening to them at each stage of their journey through the experience? Where are they? What are they seeing? What tools are they using? What are they doing?

In each of the three periods, before, during, and after, write down all the touchpoints you can think of that are part of the experience.

**FIGURE 7-1**

**The before, during, and after of experience-design**

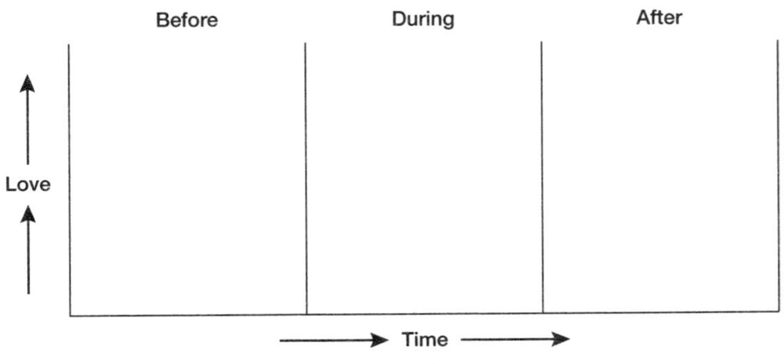

These touchpoints are your raw material for designing love in to the experience.

## 2. MMO: Focus on major missed opportunities

Arin McClune, a twenty-year veteran of neonatal nursing, joined Blue Cross Blue Shield a few years ago to help design more love in to all the practices and processes associated with maternal health during labor and delivery. Together with other members of BCBS's performance task force she was trying to create a set of standards and best practices to reduce the adverse outcomes that many pregnant women experienced—in particular, those from lower-income households.

I was interviewing her the other day and what struck me most was that amid all of the complex metrics and precise medical approaches her team recommended, some of the most powerful interventions were the simplest:

> What we identified was that, strange as it sounds, we hadn't designed our experiences around the feelings of the mother. It's inevitable that mothers-to-be become very anxious in the delivery room, and that this anxiety can have seriously negative health outcomes for her. We knew this, and yet we hadn't prioritized it.

This is a *major missed opportunity*. An MMO is not a mistake or an error that needs to be fixed. Instead, it's a touchpoint of an experience that has been left undesigned, which significantly affects the overall experience. Thus, in Arin's world of highly medicalized delivery rooms, it wasn't an error to not center the mother's feelings, but it was an MMO. Which, if they focused their creativity on it, could dramatically improve the mother's experience, and outcomes.

"Once we thought about reducing the mother's anxiety," she said, "the activations became increasingly obvious. And quite simple to implement."

"What did you do?" I asked.

> Well, lots of things. But the two most impactful were, first, moving the location of the draping so that the mother could see her baby after a cesarean section—under the previous practice, the positioning of the draping had blocked the mother's view of her newborn. We knew this must be super stressful for her, and so it was the most straightforward thing to redesign the draping so that she had a direct line of sight to her baby. We also created transparent draping so the mother could actually see the baby being born, and changed the protocol so that the baby was moved from the infant warmer to the mother's chest as soon as was medically possible so that the mother and baby could be skin-to-skin.
>
> And the second was having the nurse get down on the same physical level as the patient when talking to her. Which meant telling the nurse either to actually sit on the bed, or to bring a chair next to the bed—both put the nurse on the same eye level as their patient. We called this our Commit to Sit initiative.

In the five-feelings language, we would describe these activations as being focused on increasing each mother's feeling of harmony, of being in a room where the physical and human environment had been deliberately designed to anticipate and respond to what they were feeling. In Arin and her team's language they were just trying to do right by the mother: "So many things become obvious once you start thinking about the person actually going through the experience."

The takeaway for you is twofold: first, as Kroger's Joey did, it takes a conscious effort to put aside your own concerns and expertise, and instead experience the experience as though you were a real person going through it. When a company stops walking the stage, when they stop talking about or experiencing the experiences, and the employees of that company stop paying attention to experiences, they not only lose fluency in what might get a person to fall in love with those experiences, they actually stop being able to see aspects of those experiences that are playing out right in front of their eyes.

This is what differentiates the likes of Disney, Chick-fil-A, and Rivian from most other companies: they are constantly talking about experiences. Every associate knows that, as John Heminway found, it's not only okay to passionately advocate for a particular experience; it is what's expected. Demanded even.

Preventing passengers from feeling the thrill of staring off over the horizon wasn't wrong, exactly—it was just, in John's view, a *major missed opportunity* to create in them a certain set of feelings.

Not being clear with customers about how best to buy balloons wasn't a mistake by Kroger. It was just a missed opportunity to use that touchpoint to make a meaningful experience for, and thereby a genuine connection with, floral customers.

Mikey's servers not knowing quite what to say during their tableside sundae-making wasn't a failure—diners still ordered and enjoyed the sundae. It was just a missed opportunity to draw each diner into the world of Rustic Root. (In his book, *Unreasonable Hospitality,* Will Guidara refers to "moments of magic" that the guests find "unexpected." While such moments are clearly very welcome, the difference here is that the DLI leader is designing love in to these touchpoints in such a way that the guests come to expect them. And predict them. And it's the internalized prediction that then leads the guests to change their behavior.)

Of course, the second takeaway for you is that once you've committed yourself to walking the stage and picking out MMOs, the activations that might dramatically improve the experience often turn out to be simple and within your control. Not John Heminway's!—his activation took a decade of careful planning to make the bow safe for passengers. But his is the exception that proves the rule. Most MMOs can be acted upon immediately, and inexpensively.

Kroger just needed to rethink the sequence of the customer's balloon buying.

Mikey could teach his servers a slightly different "song" to sing at the table.

And Arin? Well, repositioning the draping, making the draping transparent, bringing up a chair, teaching nurses to meet the eye-level of the patient—these cost nothing.

But what a difference they make in the experience of the mother and in their outcomes. As a result of Arin and the team's work, they have seen dramatically improved health outcomes, including reduced cesarean rates, fewer elective early deliveries, and fewer episiotomies, all contributing to better maternal health overall.

Walk the stage, pinpoint your MMOs, use the five feelings as your creative blueprint, and you too will come up with activations that lead to more love in the experiences, and the better outcomes that follow.

## 3. MET: Maximize every touchpoint

Once you've looked through the BDA, and identified which MMOs you can design for, the next-level tool is to examine *all* the touchpoints in the before, the during, and the after, and challenge yourself to maximize each one of them.

Two things to remember here: first, every touchpoint matters.

Audi didn't think of that robocall as a touchpoint. It was, and it mattered.

The Coldplay parking lot was a touchpoint. It mattered.

The Rivian guide email was a touchpoint. So were the Jeep ducks. They matter.

Hugging a Disney character is a touchpoint. Do you know the Disney hugging rule? Look at it closely and you can see how precise and how authentic you need to be when trying to design love in. The

Disney hugging rule is not a rule exactly; it's guidance to all Disney character cast members that when a child runs up to you and gives your character a hug, you "don't stop hugging until the child stops hugging."

It sounds so straightforward, but watch any of the tens of thousands of videos of children hugging their favorite character, and all of a sudden you see the power of it. Each child throws their arms wide, the Disney character wraps them in a hug, and then waits, and waits, and waits some more until the child pulls back, simultaneously beaming and crying. It looks so natural, so loving.

But Disney didn't shape this outcome by accident. They designed it in. Inspired by Walt himself, who said, "You never know how much that child may need that hug," they thought about what the child might be feeling, and they designed a hugging touchpoint that explicitly gave the child the power to decide (a) to initiate the hug, and (b) to control how long it lasts. Of course, the child isn't aware of any of this—they just feel like they're doing something they really want to do, and they get to do it for as long as they want. It feels natural to the child, when in fact, it's all very carefully designed.

Juxtapose this with the Starbucks coffee-cup scribble tactic, and you can see why the Disney design works, whereas the Starbucks scribble falters: With the Disney hug, the child's experience is the frame of reference, and the cast member is guided in how to help each child feel, in DLI language, control and harmony. Whereas with Starbucks, the actions of the barista are the frame of reference, because they are being told what to do, regardless of what the customer may want or feel.

This takes us all the way back to return on intent. Genuine intent is a scarce, and for us humans, a very valuable resource: getting the best ROI requires careful design. With Starbucks, the intent is opaque: Why are these baristas writing these words, and how does it fit with Starbucks's story? With Disney the intent is genuine—stemming as it does from Walt himself—and tightly focused on the feelings of the child.

The second thing to remember is not just that every touchpoint matters; it's that *everything is a touchpoint.*

The grocery store's bag in your kitchen is a touchpoint. So are its receipts. So is the name-brand item in your fridge. Each one of them is an opportunity to do something intentional to foster love in the experience of that grocery store.

The line at a Disney ride is a touchpoint.

The voice you hear when you call your HR department is a touchpoint.

The boarding area of a Southwest flight is a touchpoint.

Push yourself to surface items, or actions, or communications that, in the past, you might have dismissed as simply part of the scenery. And instead look at them as touchpoints in a person's journey toward love in their heart for your company, or your product. This MET tool requires you to select a touchpoint you think might have potential . . . and then run it through the five feelings.

And please know that every single touchpoint is doing something. It is doing *work*—it is either creating or depleting one of those five feelings. No touchpoint is neutral. No touchpoint leaves you at zero. Each one draws you in a little bit toward love in your heart for the experience, or it repels you.

Look around you now.

Your car key fob is a touchpoint—and the fact that the interior of your car does, or does not, have a designed spot for your key fob is a touchpoint. Something you will intuitively make sense of in terms of the car company's view of you, and concern for you.

Your credit card statement is a touchpoint that more than likely tells you that, to the credit card company, you are merely a financial balance to be informed of, or a late payment to be reminded of.

Your nearly empty toothpaste tube is a touchpoint—one that, in its form, communicates something about whether the company cares about how much of each tube you get to use.

The programmed voice and instructions when you make that restaurant reservation represent a touchpoint, which, intentionally or otherwise, tells you something about how that restaurant sees you.

The cones used by fast food restaurants to guide you through the parking lot and into the correct drive-through line are touchpoints. If those cones are grimy, then, whether they are owned by the restaurant or not, they are noticed—subconsciously or consciously—by each customer, and some mental connection is made between the dirtiness of the cones and the cleanliness of the kitchen. In this case the connection is jarring. Disharmonious. The human wants to feel their food is pure, untainted, and the dirt on the cones reads as impure, spoiled.

As we discussed earlier in the book, we humans are all experience-makers—meaning that we pick up on *all* the touchpoints we encounter and use them to make for ourselves an experience. The DLI leader is acutely aware of this, and so is always thinking about how each touchpoint can be designed to create one of those five feelings.

The pottery seller who deliberately uses old boxes and newspapers to package their products, and then explains this as part of their stance on recycling, is designing love in. They've designed a generic touchpoint—the box—to communicate the world they're asking customers to enter, thereby shaping each customer's feeling of control.

The botanical museum that makes a sign leading into the Japanese garden reading, "We love dogs too. Just not beyond here!" is designing love in. They could have just said, "NO DOGS IN THE GARDEN." But instead, they chose words that created a small sense of harmony with other dog owners.

The manager of the kitchen store who chooses to use the store's working stove to brew warm apple cider is designing love in. They've identified the smell of the store as a touchpoint, and designed it to communicate "home" to every customer walking in. This reinforces each customer's feeling of harmony: *This place smells like home.*

The dog food company (Chewy) that, when they hear that you've canceled your subscription because your pup has passed on, credits your last month's order and sends you a small bouquet as a condolence, is designing love in. They are turning what could otherwise be an utterly dispiriting touchpoint into an experience that puts them in harmony with their grieving customer. *We know what you're feeling, and we care.*

The doctor who not only explains your condition in words you can understand, but also writes advice tailored to you for what you can do at home to get better, is designing love in. Their individualized words of guidance, prepared just for you, create in you feelings of both control and significance.

Each touchpoint is raw material for you. You don't have to tell us humans to pay attention to all these touchpoints; we do anyway: touchpoint sensitivity is the default human setting. Instead, all you have to do is start with each touchpoint in the before, the during, and the after, and then push yourself and your team to think creatively: How might we design this touchpoint to give a person a feeling of control, or harmony, or significance, or warmth of others, or growth?

Of course, not every touchpoint will be able to foster all five of the feelings all at once. However, what these five feelings will do is give you a sequenced blueprint of prompts to spur your creativity. Five feelings. Five sources of power for you and your team to shape others' behavior.

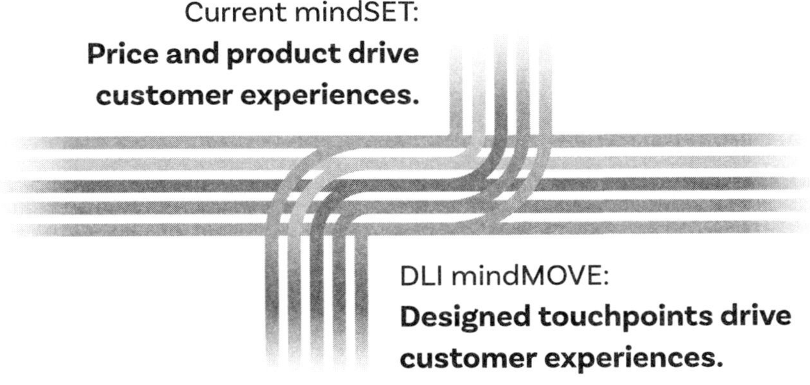

## 4. WPW: Wave your what's possible wand

At the highest level of DLI mastery, we see examples of leaders breaking free of the "That won't work here" dirge, and instead embracing the possibilities of what could be. These leaders aren't breaking rules for the sake of it. Instead, using the five feelings as their focus, they're simply asking themselves: *What's possible here? If we were intentional and intelligent about shaping people's feelings, what activations would we create?*

To open your mind to what's possible—in terms of selecting a touchpoint and maximizing the living daylights out of it—here's something for you to noodle on: Who owns your sink?

Your bathroom sink. Who owns it?

Stay with me for a moment. Obviously, at the most basic level, you do. But which company or brand have you allowed to co-own your sink with you? We've allowed various other brands to co-own other parts of our life: Apple co-owns our friendships and much of our work, since their heavily branded products are our interface. Some of us have let certain shoe brands co-own our identity as we strut down the street. We've even let certain car brands sell us signs, tools, and accessories to adorn our garage and announce to ourselves as much as to anyone else that ours is a Ford, or a Toyota, or a BMW garage.

So, who co-owns your sink?

That's the question Tom Rinks asked himself.

After selling Sun Bum in 2019, he decided to enter one of the largest and most entrenched consumer goods markets in the world: oral care. Oral care is a $44 billion market in the United States alone, and it's dominated by three players: Crest, Colgate, and Sensodyne. Together they serve 95 percent of all toothpaste and toothbrush buyers.

So why don't they own your sink? Why haven't they tried to use the sink to create a loving experience for you while you're brushing or flossing? Most of us brush our teeth at the sink. And most of us store our toothpaste and brush out of sight in a drawer or a vanity.

Our sink is directly in our line of sight whenever we're doing our oral care routine. It's a big part of our experience. And yet no oral care company has seen it that way. It's just there. Visible to us, invisible to them. Our sink is just a sink.

In Tom's brain he saw the sink as a touchpoint to be maximized. He'd noticed that none of the big three oral care companies addressed the child, other than through licensing agreements with characters such as Spiderman or Super Mario. And yet parents are constantly struggling to persuade their kids to fall in love with brushing their teeth. So, he started by creating a series of childlike characters, with toothbrushes and toothpaste flavors to match the characters. There's an alien whose toothpaste flavor is Alien's Blood (grape); a monster, Monster Slime (sour apple); a shark, Eyeball Juice (watermelon); and a cheetah named Gigi, whose toothpaste tastes like Cheetah Dust (strawberry).

These characters were all part of an intentional effort to give his customers (in this case a combination of parents and their kids) a feeling of control. To present the world he wanted them to walk into, a world so vivid and clear to which they could say a resounding *Yes! I want to be part of this world!*

Then, per MET (maximize every touchpoint), he pinpointed the sink as one of the during touchpoints—which itself was not much of a creative leap. Of course a sink is a during touchpoint. It's what the kid is standing at, or leaning on, as their mom or dad tries to cajole them into brushing.

For Tom the "What's possible?" came, as it will for you, when he reframed the sink from scenery to a touchpoint, and asked himself: *This touchpoint is doing "work." Is there any way I can use this touchpoint to create love in the heart of a kid?*

If we reverse-engineer what he did, and put in through the five feelings, the second feeling he bumped into was harmony. And so now Tom tightened his question to:

> *Is there any way I can use the sink to show the kid, or their parent, that we know how they're really feeling, and can meet*

> *them there? Can we use the sink to create an experience that will draw the family in, and perhaps even help the kid start to look forward to teeth brushing?*

They might not like brushing their teeth, Tom thought, but they do like water, splashing, and generally making a bit of a mess at the sink. *Let's run with that,* he said to himself. *Let's see if we can find a way to get really playful with the sink.*

I know. It all sounds quite odd. But this is what loving experience-makers do. They use any and all materials at their disposal as a touchpoint to bring love into the overall experience.

In this case, Tom landed on an initiative he called In-Sink Entertainment. Let's give any kid who requests it plastic figures of each of the characters, and encourage them to make little movies of the characters splashing around in the sink. Diving, or surfing, or swimming, or just making a watery, toothpasty mess.

Then let's have the kids send in their movies, hold a contest, and hand out awards at the In-Sink Oscars (significance).

Then let's post them on the Made by Dentists website and YouTube channel so that all the kids and their parents can see "people like us" doing crazy things with brushes and creatures and water and sinks (warmth of others).

And then let's create the Anti-Cavity Club and give every kid the chance to join, and get prizes for learning about, and sticking to, their daily teeth-brushing routine (growth).

Of course, the point here isn't the videos, which are just silly fun. The point is to use the sink to meet the kids (and their parents) where they are, physically and emotionally, and draw them into an experience that they love.

So, when is a sink not a sink? When we wave our what's possible wand and decide, as bizarre as it sounds, that it's a stage for a kid's playfulness.

When is a grocery bag not a grocery bag? Why can't we wave our wand and turn it into a reminder of everything that particular grocery store stands for?

When is a boarding area not a boarding area? Why can't it be the gathering place for our passengers and an audience for the fun and playfulness of our gate agents?

When is a line not a line? When we reimagine it as a ready-made opportunity to conjure in each guest a sense of anticipation for the thrill ride ahead.

In your world, open your mind to the possibility that mundane items, or actions, or emails, or interactions are all, at heart, touchpoints of an experience. Pick one that intuitively strikes you as having potential, and then wave your what's possible wand.

Find a new use for an old sink.

. . .

## What Sparks Real Change

Let's be honest: not every effort we've been part of has led to radical transformation.

Over the past few years, our DLI team has partnered with organizations across industries to design love in to their systems, teams, and experiences. Some of those initiatives launched lasting change. Others . . . quietly faded.

When we looked closely at what made the difference, it wasn't luck. It wasn't timing. It came down to a few key accelerators that were present every time the work took root—and noticeably missing when it didn't. To ensure your efforts last, grow, and move from inattention to attention to action, take note of these accelerators and design them in.

If I was advising Mikey, the restaurant entrepreneur from the last chapter, this is how I'd present them to him.

## Five Accelerators

### Name a steward

Your audience doesn't see different departments. Instead, they take in the whole experience and love it or loathe it based on the totality of the experience. To them, it's all connected.

Effective experience-design needs to mirror this holistic perspective. So it's hugely important at the outset to have a steward who is charged with seeing the experience as a whole, and who is expected to be the "Voice of the Experience." They will speak up for the audience, pulling together different departments and pulling down some of the inevitable barriers between them.

Mikey, I'd suggest you play this steward role for the whole company—and that for each restaurant, and for each companywide process, you designate an experience-steward—the single, integrating point-of-contact for designing love in to experiences.

### Start small

The best way to begin is to start small. Focus your efforts on one location or one process where all the various parts of the experience can be quickly observed and evaluated. You'll want to walk the stage efficiently, and make in-the-moment decisions about what needs to be removed and what can stay. On this small stage—Mikey, for you I'm thinking, pick one restaurant, and then one shift or one process at that restaurant—your story will be clearer, and the various people, props, scenes, and songs easier to design.

In this way your learnings will be practical, and will rise to the surface more quickly. These can then be collected in preparation for translating them more widely across your organization. Small starts lead to concentrated learnings. Everything is tightly wound together. This is critical if scaling is not to lead to diluting.

## Educate, educate, educate

Every single person, whether on stage or backstage, has a voice and a responsibility to design love in to the experience.

This all sounds well and good, and most people will be excited to step into a role that asks them to become an experience-maker. And yet, roles tend to be defined for their functional value, rather than for the value they bring to an experience. And so, most people will have become conditioned to seeing themselves as merely functional workers inside functional departments.

To break people from this mindset requires education. Specifically in:

1. Experiences drive behaviors drive outcomes.
2. Extreme positive experiences are experiences that people love.
3. Design love in to your own work, because no one can create loving experiences for others if their own work is loveless.
4. Design experiences that other people love.

Each of these demands mindMOVES, breaking free of mindsets and getting everyone to look at the world in the same way. Each of these moves is indeed doable, and vital, since consistent outcomes can be achieved only through establishing a consistent perspective.

Mikey, education of your team is the fastest route to creating this consistent perspective. Yes, no one wants to be force-fed a script. But everyone wants to be an experience-maker. Everyone wants to step into a role. Everyone wants to be a player. Teach them why, and how.

## Design a reliable dashboard

Without question, measurement improves performance. Figuring out the right metrics is critical to not only measuring the speed of the change, but also to increasing that speed.

When it comes to data, what you want most is reliable data: *Can your metrics be trusted, and are they measuring the right things?*

Mikey, if you're really into this stuff, please know that three validities combine to create a reliable dashboard:

1. Are you measuring outcomes or behaviors that are truly central to the experience—what can be thought of as *construct* validity?
2. Which of your metrics are leading indicators, and which are lagging indicators—*predictive* validity?
3. What frequency of data collection and reporting best serves the people designing and delivering the experience—*content* validity?

The combination of these three validities—construct, predictive, and content—creates reliability. The more you can push yourself to build up these three validities—refine them, sharpen them—the more reliable your dashboard will be for assessing and improving the quality of the experience. In short, you'll know for certain how fast change is happening, and where.

I would highly recommend including both DLI X metrics on your dashboard and sticking to the best practices. In combination with all your other dials, Mikey, this will add two super-reliable metrics to your experience-design dashboard.

## Critical process redesign

Despite the wisdom of starting small, on occasion you may come across a source of friction that extends more broadly.

For example, in trying to clarify the story you're telling inside one team or department, you discover there is no coherent story being told across the whole company. Instead, this one team, and all the others, are actually being told many different stories, which pull the team's attention this way and that, making it difficult for them to know what to remove from the stage, let alone what to do to tell a clearer story.

Or, in trying to decide which people to showcase in which scene, you learn that some of the people are actually not employees, but are subcontractors: you've outsourced a critical role in the experience, and therefore these people cannot easily be taught their role and their "songs."

Faced with these friction points, you may well decide that these are critical processes. And so, to leave them undesigned will act as a brake on everyone's good efforts. The speed of change will slowly grind to a halt. Not every source of friction has to be addressed immediately, but those that bring with them significant drag, degrading not just efficiency but also enthusiasm and spirit, should be called out as critical processes, and focused on.

So, Mikey, if in trying to teach your servers in Rustic Root a new "song" during the ice-cream-sundae-at-the-table scene, you discover that none of your servers has been with you long enough to learn the basics of the menu, let alone the specifics of a sundae song, you may well decide that your onboarding is a critical process. And that until you can design love in to this process so intelligently that you increase your ninety-day retention rate, you'll never be able to get traction on your "sundae singing."

Critical processes are those that catalyze a great many other experiences. Whenever you discover one that's been left undesigned, or even under-designed, call it out, scope it, and design love in to it.

## Epilogue

# A Stand in the Hallways

On Friday, July 12, 2025, the US State Department laid off 1,350 employees. All different levels. A sweeping downsizing under the DOGE administration's cost-cutting measures. In today's world of work, that's not exactly shocking. We live in a system that accepts layoffs as routine, especially in the private sector, when stocks dip, tariffs tighten, or pressure from Wall Street mounts.

But what happened that day wasn't routine.

As those being let go walked out of the building, schlepping their boxes out to the parking lot in the layoff walk of shame, something extraordinary happened: their colleagues lined the hallways. And they clapped. And they cheered. They stood in doorways and filled the entryway of the State Department. Not in protest. Not in defiance of the layoffs. But in defense of something more profound.

It was a stand against resignation. Against disposability. Against the idea that it's acceptable for coworkers to be erased quietly and cleanly, like rounding errors. They said with their clapping: *We see you. You mattered here. You still matter.*

It was a loving act. A powerful one.

And it reminded all of us: we can do the same.

We can choose to work in places that recognize people as the fundamental moral foundation. We can build companies that treat their people like people, not like parts. We, as DLI leaders, can take a stand for practices that are, at their core, loving.

These practices don't have to be grandiose or dramatic. They can be simple, specific, and unwavering. And they begin with nonnegotiables.

A company that wants to become a Design Love In company must commit to these nonnegotiables. And for those who don't? Well, that's their choice—and they most certainly can build an effective and profitable organization without them. But we should be just as clear: these are not loving companies. What they are doing is unloving—which in the short term might be something they can get away with, but in the long term will prove bad business.

Here, for you to consider, are the ten nonnegotiables for building a DLI company.

## 1. Follow the One-to-Twelve Rule

*Too many reports = too little love.*

If a CEO has more than twelve direct reports, something's already wrong. Humans thrive in small, seen groups, not sprawling, horizontal organizational charts.

In NVIDIA's case, Jensen Huang has more than fifty reports. This works for him, but it isn't loving. He can't see and know people at that scale. And they know he can't. He's designed a team size that fits his needs, but it doesn't fit any other human's needs.

Compare this to companies like Patagonia, where CEO Ryan Gellert leads with a tightly aligned executive team of fewer than ten direct reports. Smaller teams allow for depth, connection, and shared responsibility. If you're building a company and your leader doesn't know the names, the fears, the strengths, and the loves of the people who report to them, you're building a reporting system, not a relationship. And systems don't love.

## 2. No Surveillance Software

*You cannot love someone you don't trust.*

Surveillance software is a betrayal. It communicates fear, not faith. It says we don't believe you'll do your work unless we're watching. That is the opposite of helping your people to feel control, the first feeling of love. A loving company sets expectations and holds people accountable human-to-human, with consistent, one-on-one weekly check-ins. Not by watching their keystrokes.

## 3. No Recurring Layoffs to Meet Wall Street Projections

*Predictable cuts = predictable disconnection.*

This isn't about recessions or global shocks. This is about companies that include layoffs in their annual rhythm. Cisco, for example, has been restructuring roughly 5 to 7 percent of its workforce every year for over a decade. It's become normalized. It's what Cisco workers expect, and accept.

And it's worked well for Cisco shareholders: their stock price has seen a compounded growth rate of 19 percent each year for the last thirty years.

But as a practice it is fundamentally unloving. When you move people and their families halfway across the world for a new job, and then, seven months later, lay them off with no reason other than "Your position has been eliminated," this is unloving. When you lay off thousands of workers with little to no explanation to each of them as to why, and simultaneously apply for thousands of H1B visas to replace these workers with cheaper foreign labor, this is unloving.

It works on a balance sheet. But it introduces powerlessness into the system, which, as you now know, blocks any path to loving feelings, and all the good that accompanies them.

Compare this practice to companies like the $3 billion engineering conglomerate Barry-Wehmiller, where CEO Bob Chapman has made a public commitment to avoid layoffs, even during economic downturns. During the 2008 financial crisis, the company implemented furloughs and shared sacrifice, but not workforce cuts.

A loving company may face hard times, and during those times it may require reductions in the workforce, but it doesn't normalize the shedding of humans as the prime mechanism for value extraction.

## 4. Use Human Capital Management Systems Only for Payroll, Time, and Attendance

*Competency models kill uniqueness.*

Use human capital management (HCM) only for payroll, time, and attendance, not learning, performance management, skill-building, or career development.

Many of the largest HCM systems, those that stretch into performance management and skill development, treat humans like templates, as interchangeable slots to be filled. They ignore personality. They treat difference as dysfunction. They define standardized lists of competencies and skills for each role, measure each person against this standard model, and then incentivize people to ignore their uniqueness and instead try to become as close to the model as possible.

And in so doing, they are unloving. If your HCM software can't make room for human nuance, if its design views uniqueness as a bug, not a feature, it can't support love.

## 5. No AI Fakery

*AI can be loving. Deception can't.*

AI can be supremely helpful. Transparent use of it can even be loving. But when companies blur the line by making it unclear whether that email, that chat, that message is from a person or a machine, they remove control and harmony from the interaction.

Duolingo uses playful bot interactions but is always up-front that they're bots. By contrast, some banks and telecoms deploy chatbots with fake human names and headshots, only revealing the automation after the fact, or never at all. That's not transparent. It's fakery. And fakery is unloving.

## 6. No Numbered Performance Rankings

*If I'm a score, I'm not a person.*

Numeric performance ratings are inherently unloving. They flatten complexity, reducing one human's contribution to a digit.

Stack-ranking practices used at Amazon, Meta, and previously at Microsoft (known as "rank and yank") are notorious for damaging morale. In contrast, Atlassian eliminated annual ratings and introduced "performance check-ins" focused on development and conversation, not scores. A loving company doesn't rank and stack its people. Instead, it checks in weekly with each person, and these check-ins keep the leader and the team member connected, and the team member's focus aligned to the changing needs of the team, and the company.

Loving doesn't mean avoiding tough performance conversations. It means having real conversations between two real humans about recent performance, whether good or bad. This kind of weekly check-in cadence brings all five feelings of love into the interaction. It's the single most powerful and loving practice a leader can do with each team member.

And it is the antithesis of the once-a-year performance ranking.

## 7. Keep Customer Support In-House

*You can't outsource customer intimacy.*

Apple doesn't outsource its support. Neither does First Direct in the United Kingdom, which is routinely rated the top bank for customer service. Every support agent is trained in-house and located in the United Kingdom. No scripts. No third-party vendors. No automation.

On the flip side, companies like Comcast, AT&T, and many airline carriers rely heavily on offshore business process outsourcing (BPO) centers and scripted support models.

You feel the difference immediately. When your first point of contact isn't part of the company's culture, you, the customer, aren't getting cared for—you're getting contained. And you feel unloved.

The DLI leader, and the company they're building, makes customer-closeness a fundamental design pillar. To be able to give customers feelings of control, of harmony, of personal significance requires that these customer voices, and their unique challenges and frustrations, be heard. The DLI leader knows that only by attending to the detail of the customers' actual experience can they know precisely how to design love in to that experience.

## 8. Avoid Interactive Voice Response Systems

*IVRs are a convenience for the company, but a disconnection for the caller.*

A loving company doesn't begin with a machine. Restaurants, telecoms, airlines, if the first voice the customers hear is a robotic menu, you've already signaled that they're a ticket, not a person.

First Direct refuses to use IVR systems, opting instead for immediate human contact. Meanwhile, a myriad of other companies route customers through long, impersonal phone trees.

One approach builds connection. The other almost immediately breaks it.

## 9. Keep the Pay Gap Human

*A 300:1 ratio is many things—"unloving" is the most damaging.*

In the United States, the average CEO-to-worker pay ratio now exceeds 300:1. At Amazon, it's over 800:1. These numbers are so extreme they lose meaning.

Compare this with most European countries, where ratios typically fall between 30:1 and 60:1. In Germany and the Netherlands, corporate governance structures with worker representation help keep pay grounded in shared value. And in the Mondragon Corporation, a large federation of worker-owned cooperatives in Spain's Basque region, executive pay is capped between 6:1 and 9:1. They've been operating that way for over sixty years—competing globally, thriving locally, and proving that a business doesn't need to hyper-extract from its people to succeed.

A 1:50 ratio at least offers the possibility of a connection between leaders and workers. The CEO is close enough to the daily realities of each worker that they can figure out how to give each one a feeling of control in their own lives—or show that they know what each worker is feeling and that they care about these feelings, which is harmony.

A ratio such as this is loving because it keeps the CEO and the frontline team member in the same world. Whereas a 300:1 ratio disperses them to far-flung galaxies—and you cannot love what you cannot see.

## 10. Honor the Founder's Flame

*You can maximize return on intent only if the intent stays visible.*

Ely Callaway of Callaway Golf Company said, "Enjoy the game."

Barney Kroger started with, "Beware basement bread."

Tom Rinks launched Sun Bum with the simple reminder, "It doesn't have to be ours. Just wear sunscreen."

Yvon Chouinard of Patagonia said, "We're in business to save our home planet."

These weren't taglines. They were deep beliefs, and they became the North Star for everyone who joined the mission.

You can feel this kind of intent still today. At Poppi, the gut-healthy soda brand, cofounders Allison and Stephen Ellsworth share openly that they started the company not to chase a beverage trend, but to help Allison feel better after battling gut issues. At Rivian, CEO RJ Scaringe speaks not just about EVs, but about reimagining what mobility can mean for the planet, and how to build a company from scratch that reflects those values. And at First Direct, CEO Chris Pitt talks about banking with a human voice—and he still takes customer calls himself. He's said, "Our goal is to be the bank that feels like it knows you." That's the founder's intent, the founder's flame, still burning decades after First Direct opened its phone lines back in 1989.

When a company carries its founder's flame high, it gives everyone control. It defines vividly the world the organization is standing for, and asks everyone—whether customers or employees—*Do you want to become part of this world?* Sure, the vividness of the founder's flame may repel some people. Some folks recoiled from Southwest's unassigned seating experience, or Chick-fil-A's "closed on Sundays" stance—but it will also attract countless others. Its vividness will present them with a clear picture and a clear choice. It will give them control, and control kindles love.

. . .

We began this epilogue with people lining a hallway. They were clapping for colleagues. But really, they were standing up for something deeper: the belief that how we treat each other at work matters. That love has a place in business. That we are not here just to be efficient; we are here to be *with* and *through* and *for* each other. That we, the people, matter.

These ten practices are not everything. But they are a line in the sand.

If your company lives by these ten rules, you're building something powerful.

If it doesn't? It's not too late.

This is your invitation. This is your stand. This is your chance to do your part to design a DLI company, and so unleash the most powerful force in business. This is your chance to change the lives of those you lead, and those you serve. This is your chance to lead us into a more loving world.

We deserve this world.

You, as a leader, can take us there.

And we will love you for it.

# The DLI Company Nonnegotiables

Nonnegotiable #1
**Follow the One-to-Twelve Rule**

Nonnegotiable #2
**No Surveillance Software**

Nonnegotiable #3
**No Recurring Layoffs to Meet Wall Street Projections**

Nonnegotiable #4
**Use Human Capital Management Systems Only for Payroll, Time, and Attendance**

Nonnegotiable #5
**No AI Fakery**

Nonnegotiable #6
**No Numbered Performance Rankings**

Nonnegotiable #7
**Keep Customer Support In-House**

Nonnegotiable #8
**Avoid Interactive Voice Response Systems**

Nonnegotiable #9
**Keep the Pay Gap Human**

Nonnegotiable #10
**Honor the Founder's Flame**

# Index

Page numbers followed by *f* indicate figures.

# Acknowledgments

Every book is a collaborative act, and I am deeply grateful to the people who shaped, supported, and strengthened this one.

My editor at Harvard Business Review Press, Jeff Kehoe, has been a wise partner in shaping ideas into their clearest and most powerful form. His intellect, thoughtfulness, and unwavering commitment to rigor elevate every page.

To the extraordinary team at the Press—Amy Bernstein, Erika Heilman, Adi Ignatius, Julie Devoll, Jennifer Waring, and Stefani Finks—thank you for your belief in this work and for the care you brought to every draft and detail.

My agent, Jay Mandel, at William Morris Endeavor (WME), continues to be a trusted guide and advocate. His counsel and steady hand make the creative journey possible.

My love goes out to Jaqai Mickelsen, the creative genius within our company, whose imagination and instinct for storytelling continually push our ideas into new and unexpected "Hubertian" dimensions.

I am also indebted to a circle of leaders and friends whose influence helped bring the ideas in this book to life.

To Larry Emond, my old friend and fellow traveler from our Gallup days and beyond—thank you for your wisdom, your perspective, and your companionship over so many years.

To Tim Massa, whose innovative leadership opened doors to insights that will guide leaders for decades to come, thank you. And to Ann Reed and Karl Niemann, thank you for the trust and pioneering spirit you've brought to our partnership. It's rare, and lovely.

To Andrew Cathy, Susannah Frost, Cliff Robinson, and all the passionate leaders and entrepreneurs at Chick-fil-A who continually demonstrate what's possible when love becomes a guiding principle for a business.

To Nick Taylor, for his groundbreaking work in elevating mental health as a strategic business imperative—and for his friendship.

To Josh D'Amaro, for showing us all what leadership looks like when it's grounded in courage, clarity, and a genuine commitment to the people we serve.

To Lynn Merritt, whose faith in this work and passion for its promise have been energizing.

To Eli Corriveau, for his light touch, skilled eye, and talent for finding the heart in it all.

And to all those leaders who, every day, reject the mindset of "what can we get away with?" and instead step fully into their roles as loving experience-makers—your example animates every idea in this book. You inspire us all.

To Tom Rinks, whose lifelong commitment to creativity—expressed through products, brands, and experiences people love—remains a constant source of inspiration for what it means to design with boldness and heart. Thank you for all the love.

Finally, none of this would exist without Myshel Buckingham. She is the founding visionary of our company and the original spark behind the ideas in this book. Her insight, intuition, and fierce belief in the power of love to transform human behavior have shaped not only this work but the entire mission of the Buckingham Institute and LoveThat. I am indebted and inspired by her imagination, her leadership, and the relentless clarity with which she sees what others miss.

# About the Author

**MARCUS BUCKINGHAM** is a researcher focused on human excellence and human uniqueness. For more than three decades, he has been one of the world's most influential voices on what makes people thrive at work and in life. His career began at Gallup, where he spent nearly twenty years developing strengths-based assessments, including StrengthsFinder, and coauthoring the landmark bestseller *Now, Discover Your Strengths*. His pioneering research helped launch a global movement around identifying and amplifying what is best and most energizing in each individual.

Buckingham is the author of multiple *New York Times*, *Wall Street Journal*, and *USA Today* bestselling books, including *First, Break All the Rules*, *StandOut*, *Nine Lies About Work*, and *Love + Work*. His work has been published by Harvard Business Review Press and translated into more than thirty languages. As a speaker, he has delivered keynote addresses to millions of people worldwide and has advised leaders at every level—from *Fortune* 100 CEOs to global brands, such as Disney, Microsoft, Hermès, Cathay Pacific, and Kroger, to educational institutions, health-care systems, and nonprofits committed to elevating human potential.

Marcus is the founder of the Buckingham Institute, where he leads research into what makes people thrive, and of the experience design firm LoveThat, which develops tools and learning experiences to help individuals, leaders, and organizations unleash the power of love in the world.

Buckingham's work centers on a simple, transformative idea: when people discover what they truly love and design their work around it, they flourish—and so do the organizations they serve. His life's mission is to help every person identify what makes them come alive and to help every leader create experiences where human excellence can take root and thrive.